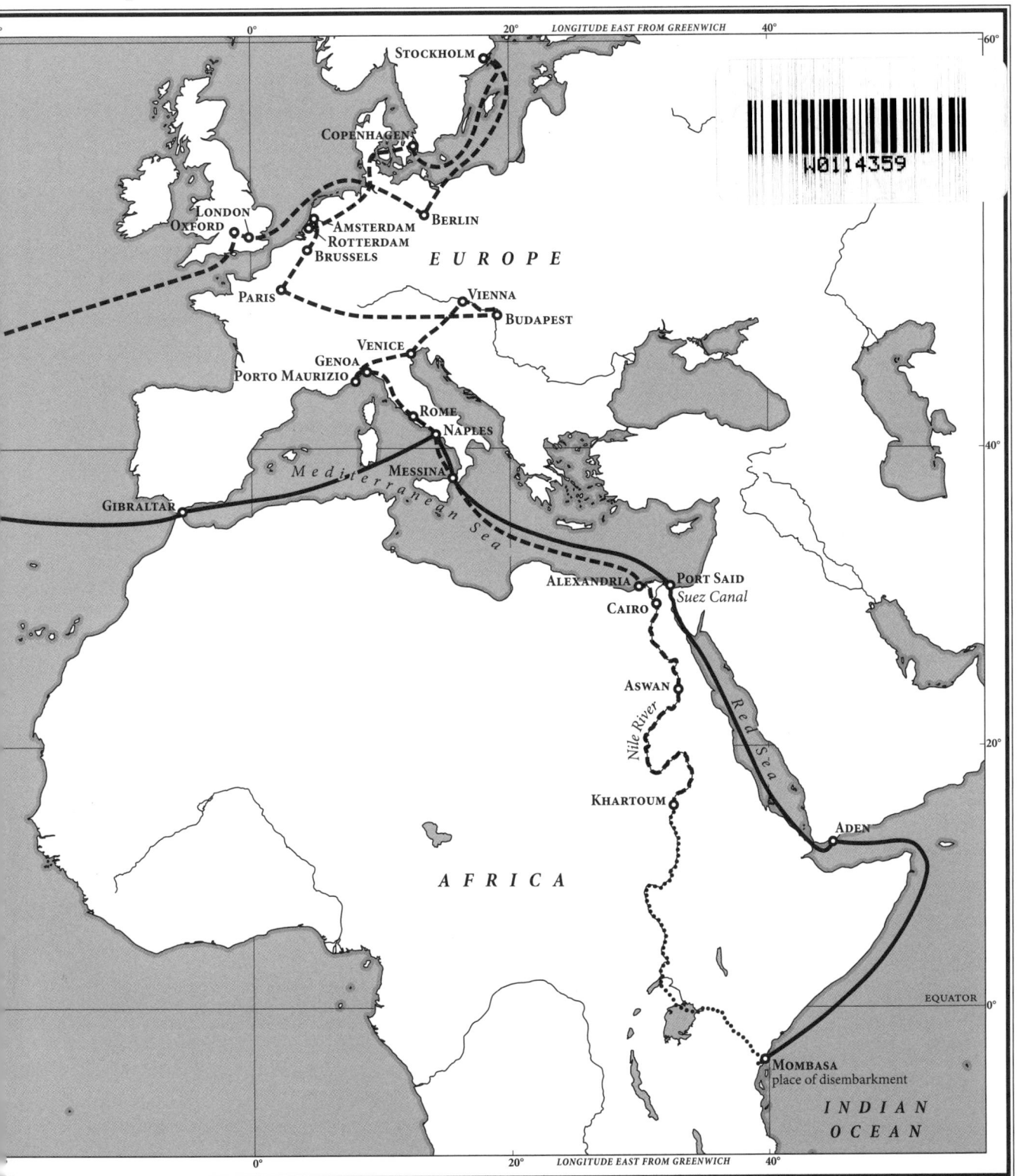

LONGITUDE EAST FROM GREENWICH

60°

STOCKHOLM

COPENHAGEN

BERLIN

LONDON
OXFORD

AMSTERDAM
ROTTERDAM
BRUSSELS

E U R O P E

PARIS

VIENNA

BUDAPEST

VENICE

GENOA
PORTO MAURIZIO

ROME
NAPLES

40°

Mediterranean Sea

MESSINA

GIBRALTAR

ALEXANDRIA

PORT SAID
Suez Canal

CAIRO

ASWAN

Nile River

Red Sea

20°

KHARTOUM

ADEN

A F R I C A

EQUATOR   0°

MOMBASA
place of disembarkment

I N D I A N
O C E A N

LONGITUDE EAST FROM GREENWICH

Theodore Roosevelt

AND THE

SMITHSONIAN EXPEDITION

TO

BRITISH EAST AFRICA

1909–1910

FRANK H. GOODYEAR III

SMITHSONIAN BOOKS
WASHINGTON, DC

Published by Smithsonian Books
PO Box 37012, MRC 513
Washington, DC 20013
smithsonianbooks.com

Director: Carolyn Gleason
Senior Editor: Jaime Schwender
Digital Imaging Technician: Bill Whitcher

Edited by Gregory McNamee
Designed by Brian Barth

This book may be purchased for educational, business, or sales promotional use. For information please write the Special Markets Department at the address or website above.

Library of Congress Cataloging-in-Publication Data available upon request.

Printed in China, not at government expense

29 28 27 26 25   1 2 3 4 5

Table of Contents

Preface

The Roosevelt-Smithsonian Expedition to British East Africa in 1909–10 represented a significant moment for American science, for America's understanding of Africa, and for the Smithsonian Institution, an organization founded in 1846 in Washington, DC, for the "increase and diffusion of knowledge." Theodore Roosevelt's role in the expedition and his 1910 book *African Game Trails: An Account of the African Wanderings of an American Hunter-Naturalist* made the safari widely known throughout the United States and around the globe. It popularized research in the natural sciences and introduced many Americans to Africa, a continent that most non-Africans little understood and frequently misrepresented. The specimens collected then numbered more than 23,000 and have long served as the foundation of the Smithsonian's East African holdings. Scientists continue to utilize them and supporting field notes compiled by the accompanying naturalists for research purposes. In addition, the photographs created by Roosevelt's son Kermit and Smithsonian naturalists Edmund Heller and J. Alden Loring were more extensive than those collected during any previous African expedition and suggested photography's potential to support scientific study.

As popular and significant as it was, the expedition was controversial in its own day. The public did not wholly celebrate the vast quantity of collected specimens, including endangered animals such as the white rhinoceros. In a dawning age of conservation and growing awareness of what the loss of species and habitat might mean, many people abhorred what they perceived as the wanton destruction of wildlife, especially by a former president. For many Americans and others abroad, especially Africans, the expedition also exemplified America's continued participation in a wider imperial enterprise and the ongoing "Scramble for Africa" by the world's great powers. As president, Roosevelt had embarked on a foreign policy unprecedented in its ambition. His postpresidential safari represented a continuation of those commitments, and many expressed concern at—and even disgust with—the growth of Western colonialism in Africa and other parts of the globe.

More than a hundred years later these controversies remain resonant, some more so than others. The removal of Roosevelt's statue outside New York's American Museum of Natural

Kermit Roosevelt, *Hartebeests*, April or May 1909

6

Edmund Heller, *A Great Candelabrum Euphorbia by Our Camp*, June 1909

History in 2022, the global campaign to ban the ivory trade, and the often-heated discourse about the practice of hunting and exhibiting exotic animals suggest that this expedition and others like it remain fraught with larger issues. In addition, the legacy of imperialism in postcolonial Africa persists as a topic that Africans and non-Africans alike continue to debate. Not the first safari by non-Africans, the Roosevelt-Smithsonian Expedition to British East Africa was nonetheless widely influential not only in popularizing big-game hunting but also in furthering attitudes and policies that demeaned Africans and denigrated their homelands. An important chapter in Roosevelt's life, this expedition highlights his lifelong interest in hunting, natural history, and exploration, while also laying bare a host of contradictory and at times inflammatory sentiments about him and other non-Africans drawn to these lands.

Foreword

LONNIE G. BUNCH III

Theodore Roosevelt's accomplishments as a naturalist and a conservationist are well chronicled. Toward the end of his presidency, when he wrote to Smithsonian Secretary Charles Walcott to propose a joint expedition to Africa that would provide "the best chance for the National Museum to get a fine collection, not only of the big game beasts, but of the smaller animals and birds of Africa," he was not being boastful. The expedition yielded the specimens of more than 160 species of mammals and 18,000 birds, plants, and ethnographic objects.

Not only did Roosevelt help build the early collections at what is now the National Museum of Natural History, but he also foreshadowed the Smithsonian's enduring connections to Africa. Today we have a bird-friendly coffee program in Ethiopia, conserve cheetahs in Namibia, and protect cultural heritage in Mali, among many other endeavors on the continent. But if we are to accurately appraise Roosevelt, we must do so with clear eyes and acknowledge hard truths about his beliefs and actions, many of which are at odds with our modern values.

Despite presenting the expedition to Walcott as purely motivated by scientific curiosity and describing himself as "not in the least a game butcher," Roosevelt was a big-game hunter who had killed 296 animals at the time and praised elephant poaching as an "adventurous" career. He also held racist views about African Americans and Indigenous people and favored the expansion of white power through colonialism. As president, he dishonorably discharged a regiment of 167 Black soldiers for a fight that saw the death of a white civilian in town, despite white officers' testifying that the soldiers had been in their barracks at the time of the fight. Roosevelt even supported eugenics, praising *The Passing of the Great Race*, a notorious book that promulgated scientific racism and served as the intellectual justification for Nazi Germany's horrific policies, writing that the book was "in grasp of the facts our people most need to realize."

Although Roosevelt held many ideas most of us consider repugnant today, he also proved capable of change. In fact, the Smithsonian expedition's most remarkable outcome may have been Roosevelt's new, more enlightened worldview. Toward the end of the nearly year-long African trip, the group of hunters, naturalists, and support staff traveled to the kingdom of Buganda, a highly advanced nation with a sophisticated economic, political, legal, and military infrastructure. As professor and author, Jonathon L. Earle wrote of the experience,

J. Alden Loring, *Theodore Roosevelt at the Head of a Safari Party of African Men*, January 1910

"Buganda compelled Roosevelt to rethink his fundamental assumptions regarding Black progress and civilization."

Though he remained a steadfast supporter of European and American colonialism in East Africa, that change of mindset was evident in his focus on civil rights when he ran for president again under the banner of his "Bull Moose" Party. Realizing his positions on race had been flawed, he spoke plainly about the need to give African Americans the benefits of full citizenship enjoyed by their white counterparts. In a 1912 speech at the National Progressive Convention in Chicago, Roosevelt hailed the gathered Black delegates who "in point of character, intelligence and good citizenship, stand on an exact equality with any of the whites among whom they sit," a reversal of his earlier notions of white supremacy. The country still was not ready for what it saw as a radical position on race, however, and Roosevelt handily lost his last White House bid.

The value of books like this one and of cultural institutions such as the Smithsonian is their ability to offer an honest, nuanced appraisal of history and the figures we venerate. Exploring the past and uncovering our unvarnished history is vital for understanding who we are, placing into context how we got here, and showing us where we want to go. Theodore Roosevelt was complex, evolving, and contradictory—in short, human. *Theodore Roosevelt in Africa* facilitates a richer understanding of Roosevelt by not simply offering us a list of accomplishments but by examining the time and place that shaped him and giving us insight into the enduring legacy he left the Smithsonian.

Introduction

In 1908, a year before he departed the White House, speculations began to mount about what Theodore Roosevelt would do after his presidency. Reports varied widely. Some thought he might write a history of his years in office, others that he might become president of Harvard University or a new educational institution in Washington, DC, being founded by industrialist Andrew Carnegie. Still others conjectured that he might seek the Senate seat of retiring New York power broker Thomas Platt, the man who helped to orchestrate his selection as William McKinley's vice-presidential running mate in the 1900 election. Despite Roosevelt's pronouncement after his victory in the 1904 presidential election that he would not seek another term, many believed—and indeed hoped—that he might campaign for reelection all the same. He seems to have considered this possibility at times, yet during this period he frequently assured the public that he had no intention of running in 1908.

Newspapers mentioned the idea that the retiring president might also travel outside the United States, perhaps even embark on a global tour. Roosevelt's interest in travel, and his love of hunting and the outdoors, were well known. Many believed that Roosevelt, after nearly eight years as president, deserved a break and time to pursue other personal interests. Given his wide popularity and bold executive style, travel might also provide his successor space to establish his own standing before the eyes of the nation. Mindful of his outsized personality, he realized that even in retirement at his home on Long Island he would continue to be a significant presence in American politics. International travel would then also take him away from these debates and leave them to others. Europe, India, Africa, and Alaska were all rumored as possible destinations. While Roosevelt made public that he had no interest in visiting the royal palaces of Europe and meeting with foreign dignitaries, as Ulysses S. Grant had done upon his departure from the White House three decades earlier, he did suggest that he might like to revisit with his wife, Edith, the European cities to which they had traveled years earlier in their marriage.

Roosevelt left unanswered most of the reports that circulated at the time. However, on March 28, 1908—less than three months before the Republican National Convention—he revealed something of his intentions to a group of close friends. In attendance at the annual meeting and dinner of the Boone and Crockett Club, held at the Metropolitan Club in Washington, the president spent the evening with two dozen leaders from the world of science and wilderness conservation. Celebrated figures such as ornithologist C. Hart Merriam, geologist Arnold Hague, and Gifford Pinchot, the founding director of the US Forest Service, were among the guests at what was part social gathering and part business meeting. The group passed resolutions that evening supporting a Senate bill to create a national bison range in Montana and another to establish Glacier National Park, also in Montana. Amid the discussion that evening with members of a club he had helped to found back in 1887, Roosevelt let it be known that he was investigating the possibility of a hunting trip to Africa. While it is unclear who leaked the report to journalists, two weeks later newspapers across the country circulated the news that the retiring president would go abroad for a year, that he did not want to be a distraction to the new president, and that he was likely to do some hunting during his time away.

Roosevelt did not publicly acknowledge the report at first. Over the following month, more details continued to come out about what the retiring president was thinking. On May 2, as he hosted naturalist John Burroughs on a birdwatching excursion at "Pine Knot," Roosevelt's country home in Virginia, the *New York Times* published a front-page article on the proposed trip. Noting that "rest and the recreation of hunting" were "minor" reasons for a journey that was to last two years, it reported that Roosevelt "intends to put himself beyond the reach of those persons who would inevitably seek, if he were within reach, to use his influence with the new Administration." Confident that William Taft, his secretary of war, would win the Republican nomination and then the general election in November, "he is determined to give Mr. Taft an absolutely free hand. If Mr. Roosevelt should remain in this country and be accessible to our citizens, everything that Mr. Taft would do as President would be discussed with relation to Roosevelt." Instead, he would go to Africa to hunt big game, "the sport which most appeals to him," and afterward to other unnamed destinations around the globe. Recalling Grant's grand farewell tour, the article concluded that "Mr. Roosevelt will avoid all that, and by spending a good part of his time in pursuit of game he will put himself out of the way of social entertainment."

Four weeks later, in early June 1908, Roosevelt stepped forward and publicly confirmed what the newspapers had been reporting for months. He and his second son Kermit, then about to graduate from high school in Massachusetts, would travel to British East Africa for a hunting trip immediately following his departure from the White House. The trip, the *Times* wrote, would "last fully a year," and "the President and his advisers [had already] begun the study of the best weapons for use against big game." While most newspapers praised him for his service to the nation and wished him well on this excursion, many could not overlook the timing of his announcement. Less than two weeks later the Republican political establishment was to meet in Chicago for its national convention. There the party's presidential nominee would be selected. Although Roosevelt had come out publicly in favor of Taft the previous fall and remained

Unidentified photographer, *Birds Collected in Egypt in the Winter of 1872–73 and Mounted by Theodore Roosevelt*, c. 1873

steadfast in supporting him through the spring, much speculation continued about others who might unseat Taft. Most especially, Roosevelt supporters championed the idea that the president might once again throw his hat in the ring. Roosevelt reaffirmed his pledge not to run, reminding supporters of George Washington's example of leaving the office after two terms. Yet he and the public understood that he had not served two complete terms, having assumed the presidency on the occasion of McKinley's assassination in September 1901, six months after being sworn in as vice president. Privately he went back and forth about whether to seek reelection, and the newspapers, noting the groundswell of support for another term, wrote increasingly about this possibility. His declaration that he was going to Africa was meant to dash those rumors once and for all, although he seems to have been undecided until the last moment.

While his planned departure date was still ten months away, Roosevelt had been considering the trip seriously for almost a year and had been actively seeking advice from experts on African travel since March. The source of his interest in Africa, however, went back to his boyhood and to a lifelong interest in wildlife and hunting. His first encounter with Africa occurred in 1872, when his family made a yearlong trip there and to Europe. Then thirteen years old, Roosevelt marveled

Julius Ludovici, *Theodore Roosevelt*, 1885

especially at the extraordinary wildlife he encountered while traveling through Egypt. Having previously begun collecting specimens at home for his own natural history museum, he gathered many bird specimens during the family's trip down the Nile River. In his youth, hunting became a favorite pastime. A prolific writer, Roosevelt wrote or edited ten books about hunting and wildlife before becoming president and published three other volumes during his tenure in the White House. He also contributed essays or forewords to numerous wildlife books by friends and associates. As celebrated as he was as a politician and a military officer, he was equally well known for his love of the outdoors. The opportunity to hunt big game in Africa was something he longed to do.

In *An Autobiography*, published in 1913, Roosevelt wrote frankly about his upbringing and his growing sense of self, and reflected that his interest in manly pursuits such as boxing, wrestling, and hunting grew out of "having been a sickly boy, with no natural bodily prowess." Admitting that he "was nervous and timid," he "felt a great admiration for men who were fearless and who could hold their own in the world, and I had a great desire to be like them." As many of Roosevelt's biographers have described, this sentiment informed not only his personal predilections but also his larger politics. The leading proponent of what he called the "strenuous life," he believed that men of all ages and backgrounds should strive to develop their bodies and to engage in virile pursuits in the military, on the playing field, or in the wild. Only through such encounters with forces larger than themselves would they escape the emasculating consequences of modern civilization. This attitude also colored his ideas about foreign policy. Although he was reluctant to rush into battle unprovoked and became the first American to win the Nobel Peace Prize for negotiating a treaty that ended the Russo-Japanese War, he was also not hesitant to threaten or engage an enemy militarily. His heroism in Cuba during the Spanish–American War and the subsequent valorization of the Rough Riders confirmed in his mind that America must exercise its power or risk losing it. Throughout his presidency he pursued an expansionist foreign policy, believing that the United States must abandon its isolationist tendencies and become engaged as a global power in political affairs beyond its borders.

Roosevelt's past hunting trips and his membership in the Boone and Crockett Club introduced him to some of the leading conservation and hunting authorities in the United States and England. While he was initially unsure where he might travel in Africa, he knew the right people to ask. During his presidency he kept up with the latest wildlife literature and corresponded periodically with leading international experts. When a group of elite British sportsmen decided in 1903 to establish an organization to promote the protection of big game around the globe, Roosevelt was elected an honorary member in its first year. Chaired by the conservationist Edward Buxton

Pach Brothers Studio, *Theodore Roosevelt*, c. 1898

and closely allied with the Natural History Museum in South Kensington, the Society for the Preservation of the Wild Fauna of the Empire had a special interest in Africa. Britain's engagement with the continent following its abolition of the slave trade in 1807 centered on exploration, hunting, resource extraction, and settler colonialism. Beginning in the mid-nineteenth century, men such as David Livingstone, Henry Morton Stanley, John Speck, Samuel Baker, and Frederick Selous began exploring its interior and bringing back stories of the Indigenous peoples and wildlife there. In East Africa, an agreement between England and Germany established territorial borders in 1886, and the founding of the Imperial British East Africa Company two years later set the stage for a new chapter of British expansion in the region.

Roosevelt came to know well members of the Society for the Preservation of the Wild Fauna of the Empire and supported their conservation efforts, as well as Britain's larger colonial enterprise in Africa. In 1905 Selous, a society member and one of the most celebrated big-game hunters in Africa, visited Roosevelt in Washington. The president had just published his popular collection of essays *Outdoor Pastimes of an American Hunter*, and the two men enjoyed trading stories of their respective hunting adventures. Roosevelt had read many of Selous's own books and, after their meeting, encouraged him to write a new memoir. He later reviewed the final manuscript of Selous's *African Nature Notes and Reminiscences*, to which he contributed a foreword, before its publication in 1908. Selous was impressed that Roosevelt's interest in hunting was genuine and that his "knowledge of wild animals was not confined to the big game of North America, with which he has made himself so intimately acquainted by long personal experience, but that he also possessed a most comprehensive acquaintance with the habits of the fauna of the whole world, derived from the careful study of practically every book that has ever been written on the subject." The two men developed a friendship then that would influence the shape of Roosevelt's African safari.

Compared to Britain's, American interest in and engagement with Africa was not as extensive at the beginning of the twentieth century. The Atlantic's broad expanse made the continent less accessible, and commercial possibilities were less obvious, especially after a group of seven European nations divided much of the continent among themselves in the aftermath of the Berlin Conference of 1884–1885. Africans resisted this act of unabashed greed and power, though they were mostly unable to deter European imperial ambitions. In the United States, the public's knowledge of and connection to Africa were largely informed by the legacy of the transatlantic slave trade. Although that trade was abolished before the American Civil War and slavery itself after it, the long history of slavery shaped perceptions of Africa to such an extent that few other details about the region reached the popular imagination. American colonization efforts, largely centered on Liberia in West Africa, were pursued at various times during the nineteenth century. Even though African Americans held a special relationship with Africa, the continent remained to

Bain News Service, *Frederick Selous*, c. 1911

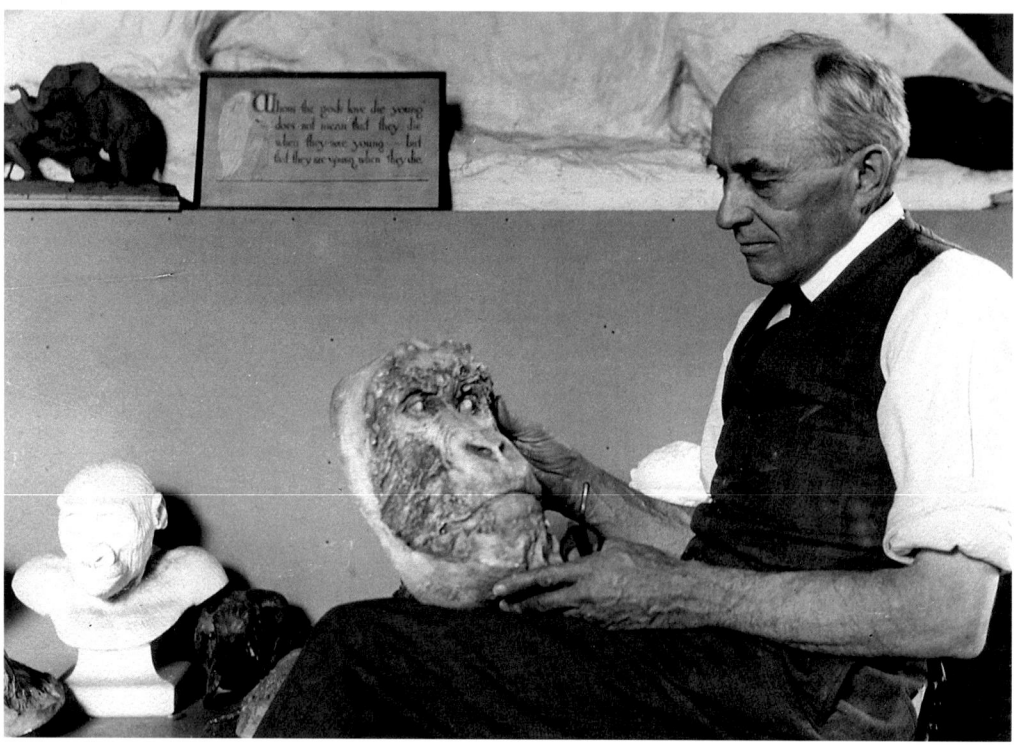

Unidentified photographer, *Carl Akeley*, c. 1922

them and others more of an idea than a concrete reality at this historic moment. American officials participated in several international summits about Africa's future in the decade before Roosevelt's trip, but few had traveled to or envisioned resettling there. To many the racist perception of Africa as "the dark continent"—primitive, inaccessible, and remote—continued to rule the day. Roosevelt shared that sentiment. As he wrote to his friend George Otto Trevelyan, a British statesman, before the trip, "my aim is to visit the Pleistocene and the world 'as it lay in sunshine unworn of the plow'; to see the great beasts like our forefathers saw when they lived in caves and smote one another with stone-headed axes. I do not want to do any butchering, but I would like to get a few trophies." Africa was then in the midst of significant political and social transformations, and many Indigenous people sought to hold out against Europe's increased authority. For Roosevelt, however, Africa was a place removed from time, a world apart from Western civilization.

American scientific study in Africa was also less advanced than that done by British and other European scientists. Whereas Europe had begun to make important contributions to mapping the continent and understanding its flora and fauna, America lagged behind. The Smithsonian

Institution in Washington had sponsored several expeditions into the interior of East Africa in the 1890s, although its research and collecting program was still in its nascent form. Both the Field Museum of Natural History in Chicago and the American Museum of Natural History in New York had African specialists and natural history collections at the time, although again their engagement with the continent remained relatively limited. Foremost among American scientists was Carl Akeley, a leading conservationist and taxidermist at the Field Museum, who first traveled to Africa in 1896. Roosevelt knew about Akeley's work and had called upon him during a trip to Chicago in 1900. On that occasion, Akeley was not there.

Instead, the two men met for the first time in November 1907 in Washington, when Akeley was en route home after his latest trip to Africa. While Roosevelt had long dreamed of big-game hunting in Africa, his meeting with Akeley seems to have provided the spark that prompted the president to begin serious consideration of the idea. In his memoir, Akeley described a dinner in Washington with Roosevelt and several of his hunting friends, including one unidentified person who encouraged him to travel to Alaska. As Akeley recalled,

> I shall never forget that dinner at the White House. I sat through course after course and did not eat a bite, for the President kept me busy telling stories of Africa. There was no time to exhaust my supply, but I believe I said enough, for as we were leaving the dining room, the President turned to me and said: "As soon as I am through with this job, I am going to Africa." "But," interposed the hunter from the north, "what is to become of Alaska?" "Alaska will have to wait," Roosevelt replied with finality. Plans for the Roosevelt African expedition went forward at once and I had something to do with their arrangement.

Roosevelt never wrote about this gathering, nor did word about the proposed African trip ever circulate publicly at this time. Yet from that evening forward he began to research the possibility seriously.

That same fall Winston Churchill, then thirty-three and serving as parliamentary undersecretary in the British Colonial Office, traveled through British East Africa on a tour to inspect new English settlements as well as the Uganda Railway, a nearly six-hundred-mile line from the coastal city of Mombasa to its terminus in Kisumu on the eastern shore of Lake Victoria. Completed in 1901 after five years of construction by 32,000 laborers primarily imported from India, more than 2,500 of whom perished from malaria and other ailments, the railroad line promised to open the East African interior to settlement, trade, and tourism. In addition to giving several speeches and meeting with British officials, Churchill also found time for some hunting. As he chronicled in a series of nine articles in *Strand Magazine* beginning in March

Reginald Haines, *Winston Churchill*, c. 1907

1908, Churchill had success on his safari, though his killing of a white rhinoceros on a protected wildlife reserve proved controversial in many quarters. The young politician enjoyed his safari in Africa yet left skeptical about England's future there. As opposed to India, where British colonization had taken root and led to increased international trade, Africa was less likely in Churchill's opinion to yield such a positive outcome.

Edward Buxton sent Roosevelt a letter in April 1908 about travel in Africa that included the first of Churchill's *Strand* articles. Roosevelt knew Churchill and disliked him, having met him in 1900 when Roosevelt was in Albany serving as New York governor and Churchill came through on a speaking tour. Buxton seems to have thought little of Churchill as well, at least as a hunter, telling Roosevelt, "though a distinguished politician, I do not think he is a very sound sportsman as I daresay you will discern if you read it." Nevertheless, the English conservationist still believed that Churchill might provide some assistance and that his route might serve as the basis of Roosevelt's own. Whitelaw Reid, the American ambassador to Great Britain, crossed paths with Churchill after his arrival back in London and learned that he was willing to assist the president. Upon receiving this news Roosevelt wrote Reid: "What you say about Churchill's talking to you is interesting; and whatever my present opinion of him, I suppose it will have to be altered if he does give me any useful suggestions!" Reid also sent Roosevelt a copy of *My African Journey*, the book that Churchill published later that year, drawn from his series of magazine articles. After telling Reid, "I do not like Winston Churchill, but I suppose I ought to write him," the president sent Churchill a short note professing that he "had read all the chapters as they came out," including "the hunting chapters and especially the one describing how you got that rare and valuable trophy, a white rhinoceros head. Everyone [in England] has been most kind to me about my proposed trip to Africa. I trust that I shall have as good luck as you had." Despite Churchill's offer of assistance, Roosevelt never pursued any substantive conversation about Africa with him.

Churchill's episode with a white rhinoceros drew increased public attention to animal reserves and hunting laws in Africa that various European nations had recently agreed upon. Meant to protect big game populations, in East Africa they largely benefited the interests of aristocratic sportsmen who wished to curtail unregulated hunting by Indigenous communities and colonial settlers. Yet, it was these same elite hunters—nicknamed "penitent butchers" by critics—who routinely were permitted to pursue big game. In the leadup to Roosevelt's trip, British officials promised the former president that they would make an exception and permit him to hunt in the protected wildlife reserves, as Churchill had done. The president was eager to match or surpass Churchill's hunting record, telling Reid, "I should consider my entire African trip a success if I could get to that country and find the game as Churchill describes it." Roosevelt continued: "The white rhinoceros is the animal I care most to get—even more than the elephant," and he promised that he would present a specimen to

the Natural History Museum in South Kensington "to show my appreciation of the way the British authorities are treating me." However, after Reid apprised him of the unfavorable reception that Churchill had received in England for hunting in the reserves, Roosevelt decided to change his plans and told authorities that he would not hunt there. Instead, he would wait until the safari reached Uganda to pursue a white rhinoceros. Reid also warned him that recent reports about the killing of this rare mammal by Churchill and others were eliciting criticism in many circles. About this concern, though, Roosevelt seems to have been unmoved.

Roosevelt was neither a stranger nor a sideline observer to the public controversies that centered on hunting big game for sport. Although most of his supporters approved and even celebrated his love for hunting, he was sensitive to critics' charges that hunters were "game butchers." In the United States, this debate manifested itself most visibly during his presidency in a series of published exchanges that became known as the "nature faker controversy." Roosevelt's friend the naturalist John Burroughs prompted the debate after publishing an article in 1903 that accused a group of popular nature writers of misrepresenting the behaviors of wildlife animals. Taking aim at books such as Ernest Thompson Seton's *Wild Animals I Have Known* (1898) and William J. Long's *School of the Woods* (1902), Burroughs accused the authors of sentimentalizing and humanizing the lives of wild animals. His targets soon fired back, not only defending their own work but also calling into question the ethics of the hunting community.

In *Outdoor Pastimes of an American Hunter*, Roosevelt waded into the controversy by supporting Burroughs. Declaring, "I wish to express my hearty appreciation of your warfare against the sham nature-writers—those whom you have called 'the yellow journalists of the woods,'" Roosevelt celebrated "the lover of nature who has trained himself to keen observation, who describes accurately what is thus observed, and who, finally, possesses the additional gift of writing with charm and interest." He continued: "It is an incalculable added pleasure to anyone's sense of happiness if he or she grows to know, even slightly and imperfectly, how to read and enjoy the wonder-book of nature. All hunters should be nature-lovers. It is to be hoped that the days of mere wasteful, boastful slaughter are past, and that from now on the hunter will stand foremost in working for the preservation and perpetuation of the wildlife, whether big or little." This sentiment epitomized his idea of modern conservation and characterized wildlife preservation projects that he championed before and during his presidency. Whether in protecting America's public lands or hunting big game in Africa, Roosevelt believed that a respectful balance between preservation and use could be struck with respect to natural resources.

Underwood & Underwood, *President Roosevelt and the Noted Naturalist John Burroughs, at Fort Yellowstone, Yellowstone National Park*, 1903

Burroughs returned the compliment publicly in 1906 in *Camping and Tramping with Roosevelt*, a memoir of trips that he and Roosevelt had made together. Remarking explicitly about charges leveled at hunters, Burroughs announced, "I have never been disturbed by the President's hunting trips. It is to such men as he that the big game legitimately belongs—men who regard it from the point of view of the naturalist as well as from that of the sportsman, who are interested in its preservation, and who share with the world the delight they experience in the chase. Such a hunter as Roosevelt is as far removed from the game-butcher as day is from night; and as for his killing of the 'varmints'—bears, cougars, and bobcats—the fewer of these there are, the better for the useful and beautiful game." Like many conservationists of the period, Burroughs saw no contradiction between hunting and wildlife preservation and heralded Roosevelt's work as exemplary. Burroughs also addressed charges directed specifically at Roosevelt, observing that "our many-sided President has a side to his nature of which the public has heard but little. . . . I refer to his keenness and enthusiasm as a student of animal life, and his extraordinary powers of observation. The charge recently made against him that he is only a sportsman and has only a sportsman's interest in nature is very wide of the mark. Why, I cannot now recall that I have ever met a man with a keener and more comprehensive interest in the wildlife about us—an interest that is at once scientific and thoroughly human."

Such praise did not quell the public controversy but instead dragged Roosevelt deeper into it. His willingness to be interviewed about the debate for *Everybody's Magazine* in the spring of 1907 opened an extended fight with William J. Long, the author of a dozen nature books and the most public voice on the other side. Long responded to the president's criticism with a scathing editorial in the *New York Times*. After refuting his claims, Long concluded: "In a word Mr. Roosevelt is not a naturalist but a grand killer. Of the real spirit of animal life, of their habits as discovered by quiet watching with no desire to kill, he knows nothing and never will learn until he goes into the woods, leaving his pack of dogs, his rifle, his prejudice, and his present disposition behind him." Though the *Times* reported Roosevelt as saying that Long was "too small to shoot at twice," Long's repeated insults and allegations drew out the president again. In September he authored a new article for *Everybody's* in which he reaffirmed his support for Burroughs's position and introduced the expert opinions of seven leading naturalists. Concluding that the "nature faker" was "an object of derision to every scientist worthy of the name, to every real lover of the wilderness, to every faunal naturalist, to every true hunter or nature lover," he identified Long again as the most "reckless and least responsible" of the group. While Long continued his criticisms into the fall, Roosevelt had made his point and declined to engage further in the debate. That said, the charge that he was a "game butcher" riled the president and influenced the way he represented his Africa safari to the larger public.

The African tales of Carl Akeley and Winston Churchill added to Roosevelt's enthusiasm for the trip, and his exchange with Long only reaffirmed his convictions about hunting's merits. He received his most useful advice, however, from a small coterie of Englishmen who were longtime authorities on travel and hunting in East Africa. Figures such as Frederick Selous, Edward Buxton, Harry Johnston, Alfred Pease, and John Patterson—all distinguished hunters and all members of the Society for the Preservation of the Wild Fauna of the Empire—responded to letters from Roosevelt about his proposed safari. He began this correspondence in earnest in March 1908, almost exactly a year before his departure from the White House. The following excerpt from his letter to Patterson, the author of *The Man-Eaters of Tsavo, and Other East African Adventures* (1907), a thrilling though gruesome account of a pair of lions that preyed on imported laborers working on the Uganda Railway, is typical of his letters. After confessing that "I cannot now decide what I shall do" after his presidency, he explained:

> It is possible that I might be able to make a trip to Africa. Would you be willing to give me some advice about it? I shall be fifty years old, and for ten years I have led a busy, sedentary life, and so it is unnecessary to say that I shall be in no trim for the hardest kind of explorers' work. But I am fairly healthy, and willing to work in order to get into a game country where I could do some shooting. I should suppose I could be absent a year on the trip. Now, is it imposing too much on your good nature to tell me when and where I ought to go to get some really good shooting, such as you and your friends had last Christmas day, for instance? Would it be possible for me to go in from Mozambique or some such place and come down the Nile? How much time should I allow in order to give ample opportunity for hunting? Would it be possible for you to give me any idea of the expense, and to tell me how I should make my preparations; whom to write to in advance, etc.? Is there anyone who outfits for a trip like that to whom I could turn to know what I was to take? I trust you will excuse me if I am trespassing too much on your good nature. It may be that I shall not be able to go at all; but I should like mightily to see the great African fauna, and to kill one or two rhino or buffalo and some of the big antelopes, with the chance of a shot at a lion.

Perhaps reflecting on his recent dust-up with Long, he concluded the letter, "I am no butcher, but would like to see plenty of game, and kill a few head."

On the same day that he reached out to Patterson, Roosevelt also drafted a short foreword to the society's annual journal, expressing his "hearty sympathy" with the group's work. Having followed closely the international dialogue about wildlife preservation, he believed that Patterson and other society members could provide him with specific answers to his different questions. As Roosevelt learned over the next few months, these men did not disappoint. They wrote often, consulted

Harris & Ewing Studio, *Theodore Roosevelt and Family on Christmas Day*, December 25, 1908

with other experts and government officials on his behalf, and sent books, articles, brochures, and maps to consult. Though encumbered with an array of political issues, including the campaign to position Taft as the Republican presidential nominee, Roosevelt made time to write almost weekly to these individuals with follow-up questions. By the time of the Republican national convention in June and the public announcement of his trip, the planning for the president's journey was well advanced. Having learned that the most favorable weather was in the summer, he envisioned departing the United States in July 1909, four months after leaving the White House, and entering Africa a month later through the port at Mombasa on the Indian Ocean. There he would board the Uganda Railway, the most efficient transportation for accessing the interior of East Africa. Then, after hunting around Mount Kenya and Uganda for six months, the party would head north to the Nile region, where he expected to spend the next three or four months before departing from Cairo. His advisers also provided him with details about specific guns, provisions, and other equipment to take and shared recommendations about guides and porters. Only the outfitter Newland, Tarlton

& Company, with offices in London and Nairobi, had published a guidebook about travel in East Africa. While he consulted it and ultimately asked the company to orchestrate the trip's logistics and furnish its supplies, Roosevelt had plenty of generous experts with whom to consult.

One of the most important decisions to make during his preparations concerned the makeup of his traveling party. In addition to selecting an outfitter and guides, he also had to decide whether he wished to travel with a companion, and if so, which person or group of individuals to invite. Many suitable partners existed; indeed, almost anyone from his "Tennis Cabinet," a close group of friends and political advisors with whom he played tennis and socialized, might have qualified. Thinking perhaps of his own boyhood trip to Egypt, he looked instead to someone from his immediate family. Though the three female members—his wife Edith, older daughter Alice, and youngest daughter Ethel—were long familiar with his hunting tales, they were not hunters and had little interest in joining the safari. Similarly, two of his four sons, Archibald and Quentin, were not suited for the trip on account of their young age. However, his two oldest sons, Ted and Kermit, were old enough. During the spring of 1908, when he began researching his plans, Ted was a junior in college and Kermit a senior in high school. Few documents provide insight into the family conversation about the trip. While Ted might have been an obvious choice because of his seniority and his impending college graduation, Kermit emerged as the son who would accompany his father. One can only speculate about the decision to include Kermit, who was only a beginner hunter and would have to set aside his schooling for at least a year. Raised on his father's stories of travel and adventure, Kermit had been interested in Africa from his earliest boyhood and seems to have been the family member most excited about the proposed trip. The choice having been made, Kermit began at once to prepare for his year abroad, while Ted finished his studies at Harvard and began a full-time job at a Connecticut carpet mill.

During the spring of 1908 Kermit was away at the Groton School, a boarding school in Massachusetts. In almost weekly letters that his father sent him, Roosevelt informed him about the latest news regarding the trip, about family affairs, and about political goings-on in Washington. Several of his advisers had warned him that certain areas were believed to be unhealthy and expressed concern about Kermit's being susceptible to malaria and other diseases. Nevertheless, Roosevelt never seems to have wavered in his decision to include Kermit. A letter to his son in April suggests his excitement for the trip, but it also makes clear that Kermit had to promise to get back to his schooling at the trip's conclusion:

> You blessed fellow, I do not think that you will have to wait until your ship comes in before making that Africa trip. If all goes well, I intend to make it soon after I leave the Presidency, and unless there is very real reason to the contrary, you will go with me. It ought to be

a very interesting trip. The only question that gives me concern in connection with it is whether letting you take it will tend to unsettle you for your work afterwards. I should want you to make up your mind fully and deliberately that you would treat it just as you would a college course; enjoy it to the full; count it as so much to the good, and then when it is over turn in and buckle down to hard work; for without the hard work you certainly cannot make a success of life. All you boys will have to earn your own livelihood, and all I can do is to try to give you a good education and to support you while you are getting a foothold; don't let anything divert you from the need of steady, hard pegging away.

In the letters he sent Kermit that spring, he often included correspondence and maps of East Africa that he had received from his English advisers. He also parceled out frequent advice about hard work and stories about personal responsibility, including a cautionary tale concerning a young American sportsman who had traveled in Africa several times but now found himself penniless and unable to hold a job. Though Roosevelt had come from a family of means, he had not earned much in his career and had in fact lost significantly after investing in a cattle operation as a young man. Financial accounting was not his strong suit, and despite being president he worried about being able to afford the trip. Similarly, while he was happy to have Kermit by his side in Africa, he expressed concern that the trip might cause his son to lose focus on the importance of finishing his education and starting a career. As he noted in one letter, "after the holiday there must be no hesitation about buckling down to hard, plodding work." He also expressed concern about Kermit's safety during the safari. His son was not an experienced hunter, and he feared that his youthful exuberance might put him in harm's way. He preached caution frequently before and during the trip, explaining that "it is no child's play going after lion, elephant, rhino, and buffalo. We must be very cautious; we must be always ready to back one another up, and probably we ought each to have a spare rifle when we move into the attack."

While they looked forward to the hunting they would do together and set aside time to practice, they also talked about other responsibilities. Of note, Roosevelt was intrigued about the possibility of documenting the trip with a camera. Photographing wildlife was increasingly common among hunters, and many conservationists of the period were advocating the use of a camera either as a complement to or a substitute for the guns they carried. Roosevelt understood photography's documentary potential, having written an enthusiastic foreword to the first volume of Edward Curtis's photographically illustrated ethnographic study *The North American Indian* (1907). Likewise, from his connection to Carl Akeley and to society members like Buxton and Johnston, each of whom had experimented with photography in Africa, he appreciated the role that the still image might play in research about the natural world. He also knew about and admired the work of the German naturalist Carl Schillings, an important pioneer in using film and photography to study wildlife. Roosevelt praised *With Flashlight and Rifle* (1905), Schillings's book of wildlife photographs taken in Africa and elsewhere, stating, "no mere hunter can ever do work even remotely approaching in value that which he has done. His book should be translated into English at once." As Americans and Europeans continued to explore and settle in new lands around the globe, the president recognized their profound impact on different human and animal populations. He saw photography, with its unique descriptive ability, as an ideal tool to record these subjects as they were first being encountered and as they changed in the wake of western civilization's advance. As British sportsman Harry Johnston acknowledged in a foreword to Schillings's book, shooting with a camera represented "the sportsmanship of the future." Many agreed with this sentiment, including Akeley, who emphasized that "camera hunting takes twice the man that gun hunting takes."

During the planning for their safari, father and son agreed that Kermit would serve as the expedition's photographer. Whether Roosevelt assigned this task to his son or Kermit proposed this arrangement is not known. Based on Kermit's enthusiasm for learning how to photograph wildlife in the following months, however, he seems to have been excited about the responsibility. Chief among those who encouraged the use of photography during their trip was Frank Chapman, an ornithologist at the American Museum of Natural History in New York. On the same day in June that Roosevelt announced publicly his plans to travel to Africa, Chapman wrote the president with news about a film he had recently made at a bird reservation that Roosevelt had helped to establish on Pelican Island in Florida. He wanted to show him the film, but he also suggested that Roosevelt bring a camera with him to Africa, stating that "such a camera would add enormously to the value of the results accruing from your trip; not only through the pictures of animal life secured, but also through those of the expedition." Roosevelt responded to Chapman at once, inviting him to Oyster Bay and wishing to connect him with Kermit, who was not yet home after the spring semester. Hearing word of Roosevelt's interest in doing photography during the trip, Chapman sent him a series of recent photographs from Africa by Herbert Lang, a colleague at the American Museum of Natural History, and suggested that Lang was available to accompany the expedition.

In the months before their departure, many people reached out to Roosevelt and various family friends about joining the safari. As on other occasions, Roosevelt declined Chapman's offer, although he did encourage his son to meet with him. In July Kermit traveled to New York, where they met for the first of several photography tutorials. Chapman loaned Kermit one of his own cameras and taught him how to use it. They also spent a day at the Bronx Zoo practicing the art of photographing animals. Chapman was an experienced photographer and demonstrated how to capture an animal in motion and at a distance. In addition, he talked with Kermit about the types of photographs that naturalists most desired and showed him the best methods for documenting dead animals. Later that fall, as Kermit was settling into his first semester at Harvard and trying out for the freshman football team, Roosevelt bought him his own camera, an amateur-friendly Kodak from the George Eastman Company. Roosevelt took an interest in Kermit's photography, saying, "I must leave all the photographic work to you." While Chapman offered to lend his own camera, the president encouraged the use of the Kodak, stating in a letter to his son, "be sure that in addition to your elaborate Chapman apparatus you take a good Kodak with you, for I think that when the showdown comes you will find that almost all that you have that is worthwhile is taken with your Kodak, and we must not slip up altogether. I think a good plan is for you to take a great number of pictures and hope that one in ten will turn out well. Then of those that turn out well we will be able to pick enough that we want." In addition to Kermit's camera, others in the expedition would bring cameras as well.

Roosevelt wanted good photographs from Africa for a variety of purposes. First, he understood them as a complement to the natural history specimens that he was planning to bring home. By picturing African fauna in their native habitats or after they had been shot, he believed that future researchers would have a fuller, more nuanced understanding of Africa's diverse animal populations. Photography was a tool that could help measure and describe the animals he encountered and the lands on which they lived. Just as importantly, these photographs also served to illustrate the trip itself to the larger world. Roosevelt was well aware of the role of the media in shaping public understanding about current events and leaders, and, during his presidency, he cultivated a specific persona to share with the larger world. He had no problem with photographers picturing him delivering speeches or leading parades, since these activities conformed to his reputation as a hard-charging chief executive. Yet he refused access to reporters and photographers who might picture him playing tennis, even though he had had a court built on the White House grounds and played regularly. During the presidential campaign of 1908 Roosevelt frequently coached Taft not necessarily in what to say but in how to say it. "Let the audience see you smile always, because I feel that your nature shines out so transparently when you do smile." He also urged Taft to give up playing golf temporarily, for though it "seems absurd, I am convinced that the prominence that has been given to your golf playing has not been wise. . . . The American people regard the campaign as a very serious business, and we want to be careful that your opponents do not get the chance to misrepresent you as not taking it with sufficient seriousness." Good photographs from Africa would remind the public of his early glory days as a cowboy in the West, as a police commissioner in New York, and as a Rough Rider in Cuba.

While he wanted an illustrated record to use alongside his own writings about the trip, Roosevelt was adamant about not allowing reporters to accompany the safari. He feared the loss of privacy and the loss of control over the story that would be told. After announcing his plans, the president came to understand the excitement for a published account of his African travels. During the same week in June in which Frank Chapman reached out about bringing a camera, Robert Bridges, an editor at New York publisher Charles Scribner's Sons, wrote the president to say that "we are immensely interested in your African project." Scribner's had published *Outdoor Pastimes of an American Hunter*, and its editors were keen to publish a photographically illustrated book about Africa by Roosevelt. Others lined up with their own offers, and the president soon realized that a significant portion of the trip's cost might be underwritten by whatever he and Kermit produced. The magazine editor Samuel McClure offered him $60,000 for a dozen articles or $100,000 for twenty articles and proposed to pay Kermit $100 per article for use of his photographs. Robert Collier of *Collier's* magazine also came forward and offered $100,000 for an unspecified number of articles and suggested that he would step aside and allow Scribner's to publish the book. In July Roosevelt decided to partner with Scribner's in part out of loyalty to the publishing house, but also on account of its literary reputation. The publisher would pay $50,000 for twelve articles to appear in *Scribner's Monthly* and agreed to publish a book that brought together the series. During this same month, Roosevelt also announced that after leaving the White House he would become a contributing editor at *The Outlook*, for which he would be paid $12,000 annually for political articles and editorials.

A yearlong safari in Africa was not inexpensive, and Roosevelt insisted that government funds should not be used to underwrite his and Kermit's travel. These writing deals eased his mind that he would be able to cover the trip's costs without compromising either the family's financial situation or his reputation for fairness. He explained his thinking about accepting Scribner's offer at the time with his friend Henry Cabot Lodge: "It is very hard to strike the happy middle between being quixotic in such a matter, on the one hand, and, on the other, following a course which is not quite proper for an ex-President whose reputation is what I hope mine is. I want to make money, but I cannot afford to make it in any way that is not exactly in accordance with my ideas." Regarding his arrangement with *The Outlook*, he told the Massachusetts senator that it "is of all the publications the one that comes nearest to representing my convictions, and its editors, although I do not always agree with them by any means, are sincere, patriotic, painstaking men, who always try to practice what they preach." Ever desirous to uphold his personal convictions, Roosevelt was also pragmatic enough to complete an arrangement that enabled him to move forward without delay.

While these funds might go far in supporting his own travel, he also had the challenge of identifying resources to pay for what he was coming to learn was an ambitious undertaking. Collecting, preserving, and shipping natural history specimens was a costly, labor-intensive business, and early estimates suggested that he needed significantly more financial support than he could expect from Scribner's and *The Outlook*. He also needed expert assistance in the field. Roosevelt was unclear initially about where he might place the animals he and Kermit shot and who would prepare the specimens. While his British advisers might direct him to good hunting guides and an outfitter, he was not inclined to deposit the results of his year's safari with a British institution. Perhaps he might provide a small number of specimens to the Natural History Museum in South Kensington in gratitude for the help that many well-wishers in England provided, but he recognized the importance and value of placing the bulk of the collection with an American museum. Questions about which institution to work with and how funds might be raised to support this work were largely unanswered at the time he announced his intention to organize a trip to Africa.

The day after Taft's nomination was secured at the Republican national convention in Chicago, Roosevelt began to explore some possibilities. Although he was a native New Yorker and had a long-standing connection with the American Museum of Natural History and its director, Henry Fairfield Osborn, he reached out instead to the Smithsonian Institution. As a government-supported museum and research organization in Washington, the Smithsonian was a more appropriate partner in Roosevelt's eyes for a man who had spent the last eight years in the White House. While its scientific program and natural history collections were less advanced than those at the American Museum, Roosevelt had consistently shown an interest in the Smithsonian. He helped it to acquire Charles Freer's outstanding collection of Asian art, enlisted its scientists in researching the lands in the Panama Canal Zone, and signed the bill authorizing the construction of the National Museum of Natural History. Believing that his African specimens might serve as a foundational collection in this new building, Roosevelt wrote to the Smithsonian's secretary, Charles Walcott, on June 20 and outlined his proposed trip:

> Now, it seems to me that this [trip] opens the best chance for the National Museum to get a fine collection not only of the big game beasts, but of the smaller mammals and birds of Africa; and looking at it dispassionately, it seems to me that the chance ought not to be neglected. I will make arrangements in connection with publishing a book which will enable me to pay for the expenses of myself and my son. But what I would like to do would be to get one or two professional field taxidermists, field naturalists, to go with us, who should prepare and send back the specimens we collect. The collection which would thus go to the National Museum would be of unique value.

Except for "a very few personal trophies of little scientific value which for some reason I might like to keep," the whole collection would go to the Smithsonian. Roosevelt felt that he had found a perfect match, given the new building and the relative paucity of the institution's African collections. Of course, if Walcott was reluctant to participate, he suggested that he could also

Scherer Studio, *Charles Walcott*, 1914

approach the American Museum in New York, though "as ex-President, I should feel that the National Museum is the museum to which my collection should go."

While Roosevelt's offer was certainly generous, there was much that he sought in this arrangement. First, he hoped that the Smithsonian might provide or connect him with several naturalists and taxidermists who could accompany the safari and prepare the specimens for transport. He also sought the Smithsonian's help in locating funds to underwrite a significant portion of the trip. Having determined not to ask for financial assistance from Congress, he thought that Walcott could be valuable in raising this money. As important, Roosevelt wanted his expedition to have the imprimatur of a respectable scientific organization. Concerned about charges of "game butchery," he wished the public to know that his trip was being conducted in a legitimate fashion and that it would ultimately serve to broaden public understanding of the natural history of Africa. As he noted in a letter to Henry Cabot Lodge, "I would a great deal rather have this a scientific trip, which would give it a purpose and character, than simply a prolonged holiday of mine." Writing on the same day on which former president Grover Cleveland passed away, he also confided his feelings about such a trip at this time in his life. Explaining that "I am no longer fit to do arduous exploring work," he confided, "this will probably be about the last time that I shall be fit even for the moderate kind of trip I have planned. But it seems to me that there is something worth doing to be done along the lines I have laid out—something that is still the work of a man of action; and I should like to remain a man of action as long as possible." Lodge supported the trip, believing it to be an ideal exit strategy from the White House.

Walcott had just left Washington for three months of fieldwork in Montana and the Canadian Rockies when Roosevelt's letter arrived. Cyrus Adler, the acting secretary, received it instead and immediately telegraphed Walcott. Before hearing back from him, Adler answered the president: "Without anticipating his decision I feel that I am justified in saying that the men and the money necessary will be forthcoming without Congressional action." He also mentioned that "it may interest you to know that just before leaving, Secretary Walcott was discussing with me the then newspaper report of your intended trip to Africa, and we both expressed the hope that in some way it might be possible to secure what collections you would make for the National Museum." Several days later Walcott wrote to confirm what Adler had suggested. He was happy for the Smithsonian to serve as a partner and pledged several naturalists and $30,000 for a special fund to be collected by private subscription. Upon learning about his publishing deal with Scribner's, he also agreed to honor Roosevelt's request that the naturalists not publish anything until after his own articles had come out. Everyone seemed to have been satisfied with this arrangement, including Edith Roosevelt, who expressed relief to hear that the specimens were headed to Washington. As her husband explained to Lodge, she "felt she would have to move out of the house if I began to fill it full of queer antelopes, stuffed elephants, and the like. As a matter of fact, I don't want any more trophies."

After confirming this partnership, Adler and other Smithsonian officials began to assemble a team of naturalists and taxidermists to assist the safari. Though many wished to join, the number of American scientists who had knowledge of or had worked in Africa was relatively small. Edgar Mearns was one of the first men to be selected. Two years older than Roosevelt, he had recently retired as a lieutenant colonel in the US Army. A bird specialist and one of the cofounders of the American Ornithologists Union, he had traveled extensively outside the United States with the military and as a naturalist. Because of Roosevelt's own interest in birds and his eagerness to collect a range of natural history specimens, Mearns was an attractive candidate, although he had never traveled to Africa. What made him especially valuable, however, was that as a former military surgeon, he could provide the type of medical assistance the expedition required.

Adler also identified and invited Edmund Heller in short order. Twenty years younger than Mearns, Heller specialized in large mammals as a curator at the Museum of Vertebrate Zoology at the University of California at Berkeley. He had traveled twice to Africa, most recently the year before with Carl Akeley on an expedition sponsored by the Field Museum. Despite his relatively young age, Heller was recognized as an African expert. The third and final naturalist to be selected was J. Alden Loring, a specialist in small mammals who had worked on previous Smithsonian scientific expeditions. Whereas the appointments of Mearns and Heller were finalized by October, Loring was not identified and invited until December.

Roosevelt corresponded and met with Henry Fairfield Osborn throughout the summer and fall, but Smithsonian officials did not offer a position to someone from the American Museum. Neither did they reach out to Carl Akeley of the Field Museum, whose African stories at the White House had so captivated the president. Institutional rivalries may have informed the selection process. However, because the American Museum of Natural History was organizing its own scientific expedition to East Africa that same summer, to be led by Akeley, it is likely that the Smithsonian was simply interested in recruiting the best people who were then available. Aware of Akeley's expertise, Roosevelt did invite him to the White House in November, where the two men enjoyed a productive conversation. They would meet again a year later in Africa when the paths of the two expeditions intersected.

With the expedition's roster now largely complete and the outfitter services of Newland, Tarlton & Company reserved, Roosevelt and Kermit now spent more and more time tending to details about equipment to bring and routes to take. As Kermit later recalled, his father wrote him nearly weekly during his time at school, and "almost every letter brought some reference to preparations." Little was left to the last minute or to chance. One topic about which the president was especially concerned regarded the proper firearms to use and their safe transport to Africa. Through the summer of 1908 he corresponded regularly with officials at the Winchester Gun Company and other sportsmen and firearm manufacturers. After several months of research and advice he finally settled on four guns: a Springfield .30 caliber rifle; a Winchester 405 lever-action repeating rifle; a Fox twelve-gauge shotgun; and a Holland & Holland 500/.450 double-barreled shotgun. A group of more than fifty British sportsmen led by Buxton and Selous presented this last gun to Roosevelt as a gift "in recognition of his services on behalf of the preservation of species by means of national parks and forest reserves." Roosevelt also secured guns for Kermit, including a Winchester rifle and a Rigby shotgun lent to him by John Jay White, a friend from New York who had used it on a recent African expedition. Practice with these different guns began at once, though nothing could approximate the safari itself. Likewise, arrangements for the transport of the guns and ammunition were also put into place.

In assembling equipment and provisions lists, many confidants sought to provide advice. According to Kermit, the initial supply lists "prepared by his friends in England were drawn up on a presidential scale with champagne and pâté de foie gras and all sorts of luxuries." For reasons both personal and financial, however, Roosevelt eschewed such extravagance, preferring instead more common American staples such as baked beans and canned tomatoes. "Father always retained the appreciation of canned tomatoes gained in the early ranching days in the West. He would explain how delicious he had found it in the Bad Lands after eating the tomatoes to drink the juice from the can." Similarly, although he sought advice from individuals, he was reluctant to accept donated merchandise from companies and avoided endorsing any specific products. When Ezra Fitch, the president of the outdoor supply business Abercrombie & Fitch, wrote him in November about naming their new line of camping tents after him, Roosevelt rejected the idea. Several weeks later, he wrote Fitch again after noticing that the company was publicizing his trip in one of their sales catalogues. Despite Abercrombie & Fitch's significant role in supplying the safari, he demanded that they remove all such notices in future catalogues. The president also declined free passage to and from Africa from a steamship company and later turned down a film company's offer to underwrite the whole trip. Concerned about his reputation, he avoided any relationship that the public might construe as a conflict of interest.

Roosevelt's preparations extended beyond guns, tents, and food rations. He also devoted considerable time to gathering a collection of books he could bring on the trip. A voracious reader, he saw this library as an important staple. "He wanted a certain number of volumes mainly for the contrast to the daily life," Kermit later commented, noting that his father had enjoyed reading British poets such as Algernon Swinburne and Percy Shelley during his ranching days in the West "because they were so totally foreign to the life and the country." Working with the Washington bookseller W. H. Lowdermilk & Company, Roosevelt assembled a collection of sixty volumes that ranged widely in subject and time period. From Homer's *Iliad* and *Odyssey* to Mark Twain's *Huckleberry Finn* and *Tom Sawyer*—with the Bible, Shakespeare, the Federalist Papers, and six volumes by Sir Walter Scott also included—the library became the source of much entertainment to him and to a curious public that scrutinized his choices. To ensure that the books would hold up throughout the safari, he asked John Loomis, the managing partner at Lowdermilk, to bind the volumes in durable leather. Loomis selected compact editions and had the page margins trimmed away to keep the weight and size to a minimum. To carry the so-called Pigskin Library, the president's younger sister, Corinne Robinson, presented him with a custom-designed, rustproof, metal carrying case, which weighed fifty-five pounds when fully packed. Roosevelt had learned earlier that sixty pounds was the maximum weight his African porters could carry over an extended period, and he and Loomis refined the library and its carrying case to get under that limit.

In preparing for the trip, Roosevelt read widely the accounts by prominent hunters and the reports of leading naturalists. While he came to familiarize himself with the flora and fauna of the African continent, he was much less knowledgeable about the Africans whom he would encounter. Because informative literature on the subject was relatively limited, he had few sources to consult. Despite this, he expressed little curiosity about the different Indigenous communities in East Africa. His interest centered on hunting and specimen collecting, not the peoples of Africa. Romantic narratives by authors such as Rudyard Kipling shaped Roosevelt's understanding about the native peoples in the British colonial empire. Like most Western travelers in Africa or India at the time, he saw them as primitives who provided little beyond manual assistance.

This ignorance and lack of curiosity were characteristic of the myopia that typified attitudes about race held by most Europeans and Americans of the period. Roosevelt had made history by inviting the educational leader Booker T. Washington to the White House in 1901—the first time that an African American had been invited to dine as a guest with an American president. Yet, during his administration, he had only cursory knowledge of or interest in the welfare of African Americans. Despite being a champion of many progressive reforms, he believed that racial progress depended solely on education, and therefore he supported figures like Washington while largely ignoring other voices. Political and social equality might be a goal, though he believed that it was not something that could be solved through legislative action. As Roosevelt told a gathering of African American students at the fortieth anniversary ceremonies at Howard University in January 1908, "go out among your people and uplift them with your example and your assistance; work, steady, strive to win the respect of yourselves and your neighbors." Only through such work over time would the problem of race in America be overcome.

Roosevelt's preparations continued throughout the busy fall election season. While playing an active role in supporting Taft's election campaign, he also devoted considerable time to refining his plans. As much as he wanted to finalize them, once a travel route was in place he began receiving a new series of invitations from different individuals and groups in East Africa. In some instances he simply turned them down, including a generous offer from authorities in German East Africa for him to hunt in their territory. After consulting with Buxton, he responded politely, saying that he had decided to limit his travels to British-held territories. Representatives from Methodist and Presbyterian missionary organizations in Africa also reached out to him, and although he was initially noncommittal, he ultimately agreed to visit missions along the way. The president also received invitations from many private British citizens who owned properties close to his proposed route or in Nairobi. While he professed a desire for privacy, Frederick Selous explained to him in a letter that "you will not be allowed to go quietly to [Sir Albert] Pease's farm without first showing yourself to the citizens of Nairobi. With the exception of the King of England, there is no man on earth whom they would be so delighted to meet and do honor to as yourself, and public opinion will probably be so strong that you will have to bow to it and put up with the inevitable receptions and banquets which you will find has been arranged for you, before you can start on your hunt." In the end, Roosevelt accepted several offers from private individuals, in part out of

American Press Association, *Theodore Roosevelt Delivers a Speech, with Booker T. Washington and Other Men Sitting on a Stage, Tuskegee, Alabama*, October 24, 1905

friendship, but also because their homes were often the only comfortable accommodations in a particular region. And even though he initially thought about simply passing through Nairobi, it would become his de facto headquarters during his time in East Africa.

The invitations were not limited to opportunities in Africa. Roosevelt was a much-admired world leader, and many people in Europe and beyond hoped that he might make a side trip to their countries after his African safari. In previous months he had said repeatedly that he was uninterested in touring the capitals of Europe after his presidency and "that it would take ten strong yoke of oxen to drag me thither." In August, however, an invitation from Oxford University chancellor George N. Curzon to deliver the annual Romanes Lecture got him to rethink his plans. Begun in 1892, the Romanes Lecture was one of Britain's most prestigious public lectures in the arts and sciences, having featured in previous years such leading figures as Prime Minister William Gladstone and evolutionary biologist Thomas Huxley. Roosevelt's reply to Curzon suggests his change of heart:

> Your letter relieves me from rather a quandary. Now there are many friends whom I have in England whom I should really like to see; but I have rather a horror of ex-Presidents traveling around with no real business. . . . If I could make the sovereigns and leading men of each country understand that I did not expect any attention and would be only too glad to be left to my own resources and be permitted to call upon the people I already knew and a very few others whom I would like to know, why that would be all right; but to make a kind of mock triumphal procession would offer about as unattractive an outlook to me as could be imagined. . . . This invitation gives me exactly the justification I require!

While he had hoped to stay out of the public eye, his acceptance of Curzon's offer prompted numerous other invitations to lecture and to visit with leaders in various European countries. He claimed initially to be uninterested in such attention, but eventually he agreed to extend his trip. Besides his lecture at Oxford, he added major speeches at the Sorbonne in Paris, before German Kaiser Wilhelm II in Berlin, at the Nobel Peace Prize ceremony in Sweden, and finally at Guildhall in London. Many European leaders also wished to meet for discussions about foreign affairs or simply to go hunting or pursue other recreational activities. Roosevelt considered for a short time the possibility of traveling around the world after receiving an invitation to visit from the prime minister of Australia, but he ultimately declined that option. On top of his many responsibilities during the closing months of his presidency, he now had multiple lectures to prepare before he departed and much additional correspondence to answer. Whereas he had wanted initially to spend an extended period with Edith vacationing in Europe after his safari, these plans had now changed.

As the presidential election drew near, Roosevelt was in a reflective mood. Looking back, he was proud of the agenda he had championed as president, often in the face of severe opposition from the Democrats and at times from within his own party. About the future, he recognized that he faced a momentous transition as he returned to being a private citizen. The Africa trip would delay his return to Oyster Bay and gave him something on which to focus during his final months in office. Yet it also made him uneasy at times. He was especially anxious about separating from Edith for such an extended period. Writing to British diplomat Cecil Arthur Spring Rice, a friend, in September, he acknowledged that "I feel excessively melancholy at being separated for so long from Mrs. Roosevelt, and I shall be so homesick, especially when, as I suppose will be the case, I have a slight attack of fever or something of the kind, that I shall not know quite what to do with myself." Nevertheless, he remained "convinced that it is the wise thing for me to go; and also I freely admit that I am looking forward to the trip!"

In October Roosevelt celebrated his fiftieth birthday, and although he would be the youngest former president in American history, various past injuries made him aware that he was likely to be less of a hunter than he had been in the past. In particular, his eyesight was poor, especially in his left eye, owing to a recent boxing injury. For this reason he brought to Africa nearly a dozen pairs of eyeglasses. Also of concern was his left leg, which had been injured six years earlier when an electric trolley car accidentally rammed his carriage during a visit to Pittsfield, Massachusetts. A great walking enthusiast, Roosevelt was thereafter slowed by this injury and the operation that followed it. He reinjured this leg in a horse-riding accident six months before his departure and expressed for a moment genuine concern about being able to make the Africa trip. Although he wished to maintain a vigorous exercise regime and to practice shooting regularly, these accidents limited his physical preparations.

Kermit's well-being in Africa also continued to trouble him. Because his son had never been involved in a hunting trip of this scale and length, Roosevelt worried that his enthusiasm and inexperience might get him into a dangerous situation. In frequent letters he shared hunting lessons and warned about the trouble that might befall him and others if caution was not observed. He was also anxious about Kermit's health and explicitly told him that he would be sent home at the first sign of illness. Letters from his advisers in England did little to ease his mind. According to Whitelaw Reid, in a letter written a month before their departure,

all the authorities I have consulted say that for a man in such vigorous health as yourself, of your years, and with a fair amount of prudence, the African journey is all right. They do say, however, that with a boy under twenty very special care is necessary on a number of points in which few boys are likely to be careful, unless they are constantly reminded. The most vital thing, some

East Africans told us, is to avoid being bitten by mosquitos, which, in their opinion, carry the dangerous fevers. Others dwell on the great danger of taking violent exercise in the middle of the day, and the still greater danger of coming in heated in the afternoon and enjoying the cooling breezes outside, as a healthy American boy would be sure to want to do. What I am afraid of is that when you get out there nobody will be willing to make you uncomfortable by such warnings, and that in consequence the boy may commit some imprudence without really realizing it.

At least initially, Roosevelt would keep a close eye on Kermit's every action while in Africa.

Preparations were also underway in East Africa in advance of Roosevelt's arrival. While the Nairobi-based safari outfitter Newland, Tarlton & Company oversaw all elements of the expedition, including labor, equipment, and supplies, British government authorities were also making plans. After 1895 much of the territory through which Roosevelt and his party would travel was overseen by the East African Protectorate under the authority of the British Colonial Office. Most Africans opposed the usurpation of their authority, though little violence had ensued between British colonizers and the Indigenous peoples of this region. Yet tensions remained in 1909, especially among the Kikuyu, who resented the British takeover. At the start of the year the protectorate was without a governor. To prepare for Roosevelt's coming, authorities installed Frederick J. Jackson, a former administrator for the Imperial British East Africa Company and a noted naturalist, to serve as acting governor. Jackson and other British officials oversaw final preparations for a lavish welcome in Mombasa, where Roosevelt and his party were to come ashore, and worked to ensure that their journey through the territory would proceed uninterrupted.

By the time of the presidential election in November, Roosevelt had finalized most of the trip's details. A departure date in March had been selected, steamship tickets had been purchased, the roster of safari companions had been secured, and a draft of the African itinerary was set. At this point he had shelved most of his presidential initiatives and begun the process of transitioning out of the White House. William Howard Taft's convincing victory at the polls pleased him not only because his friend was going to succeed him, but also because it suggested the American public's continued support for his political agenda. Knowing Taft as he did, he believed that his policies and priorities would remain at the forefront of the national debate. In a letter written to him shortly after the election, Taft was not hesitant to single out Roosevelt as one of two key figures in his victory: "The first letter I wish to write is to you, because you have always been the chief agent in working out the present state of affairs, and my selection and election are chiefly your work. You and my brother Charley made that possible, which in all probability would not have occurred otherwise. I don't wish to be falsely modest in this."

While the stage was now set for Taft, Roosevelt remained busy with presidential duties during the four-month interval before the inauguration in March. Many of his activities were simply

41

Pach Brothers Studio, *William Taft*, 1908

perfunctory, though several had special personal meaning to him. In February he traveled to Kentucky to give a speech at Abraham Lincoln's boyhood home on the hundredth anniversary of the former president's birth. Lincoln was the president whom Roosevelt most admired, and he enjoyed the opportunity to celebrate his legacy. He wrote Kermit the day after his speech, describing the crowd as "a fine audience of Abraham Lincoln's 'plain people'; on the whole, strong, shrewd, kindly faces." About his reception, he continued: "they greeted me in the nicest possible way, evidently feeling that I was their President and had tried my best to represent their interests." He returned to Washington just in time to host the North American Conservation Conference at the White House, an event organized by Gifford Pinchot, his administration's leading advocate for wilderness conservation. During the closing months of his presidency, several leading conservationists, including John Burroughs and John Muir, wrote to him to express their gratitude for Roosevelt's work in this area and to extend their best wishes on his upcoming trip.

Finally, a week before Taft's inauguration, Roosevelt made his last trip outside Washington as president to attend the homecoming of the so-called Great White Fleet after its around-the-globe voyage. Launched fourteen months earlier, the fleet comprised sixteen battleships. This peacetime maneuver was deemed wasteful and an act of belligerence in many circles, but Roosevelt, who had previously served as its assistant secretary, saw it as an opportunity to demonstrate the US Navy's growing capability. Having overseen the acquisition of new territories beyond the nation's continental borders during his presidency, he hoped to show that it could protect these lands as well as enforce new and existing treaties with foreign countries. Controversial then and more so today, his impulse for colonial expansion mirrored similar projects enacted by other nations, especially in Europe. On hand at Hampton Roads, Virginia, the president celebrated the fleet's return. Recalling its significance years later, Corinne Robinson explained: "My brother, the year before, had sent the great American fleet around the world, an expedition discountenanced by many, and yet conceded later to have been one of his most brilliantly conceived strategic inspirations. 'In time of peace, prepare for war,' said Washington, and Theodore Roosevelt always followed that maxim."

The exiting president enjoyed these gatherings, where he could celebrate heroes or achievements of his administration. While many in the press tended to be complimentary of him and his presidency, Roosevelt understood that reporters had their own agendas and were often interested in covering him solely because he was the president and because articles about him sold newspapers and magazines. Those that also included newsworthy photographs were especially valuable, and a new generation of easy-to-use handheld cameras led to an explosion of photojournalists covering American politics. Roosevelt learned to adapt to this change and was generally successful in using the news media to his advantage. That said, when reporters reached out again seeking permission to follow him to Africa, he firmly refused their requests.

This quarrel with the press had begun not long after his travel plans were first announced. From the beginning, Roosevelt was hesitant to share details of his itinerary with even the most trusted members of the media and publishing world. As he told Robert Bridges, his editor at Scribner's, "I have tried to keep the exact locations where I am to hunt very vague in the public mind, and the times also, because otherwise there is always the chance that we may have trouble with enterprising apostles of sensationalism."

With his departure nearing, he received an increasing number of inquiries from reporters and photographers. Many suggested that their presence would not lead to a rash of sensational stories but would in fact help to prevent such articles. They reasoned that magazines and newspapers were going to write about the safari regardless of whether Roosevelt was willing to cooperate. By accepting a select few journalists to accompany him, he would be better assured that the story was at least accurate. The president refused to budge. In December he wrote to Melville Stone, the general manager of the Associated Press, to inform him of his feelings on the issue. Arguing that he would then be a private citizen, Roosevelt explained that his affairs were his own business. "After I reach the wilderness of course no one will be with me, and if anyone pretends to be with me or pretends to write concerning what I do, his statements shall be accepted as, on their face, not merely false but ludicrous." In closing, he asked for Stone's assistance: "Now don't you think that we can get the newspaper press of this country to acquiesce in this view and leave me alone when I am out of office and have left the country? Can't you make the request of newspapers generally, by circular or otherwise?"

Like other journalists, Stone was unmoved by his plea and responded, "it is utterly impossible for any man who has occupied the conspicuous relation to the world that you have to drop into private life and obscurity at his own will." He continued: "I can well understand your desire in the matter, and so far as I am concerned shall be glad to do anything in my power to meet your wishes. But privacy in the matter is impossible. Such an appeal as you suggest would in my judgment hurt rather than help." Not willing to relent, Roosevelt wrote Whitelaw Reid seeking the assistance of local authorities in East Africa to prevent the press from "getting up a caravan and trying to follow me." He also wrote Lawrence Abbott, his editor at *The Outlook*, whom he had previously invited to join him on the ocean voyage from New York to Mombasa, and said that his company was no longer welcome. Apologizing for taking back his earlier invitation, he explained that "I don't want any people able to say that I am responsible for any newspaper man or magazine writer accompanying me on my trip." Though Abbott understood Roosevelt's message, the press's desire for access remained an issue throughout the expedition.

Underwood & Underwood, *The Return of the Great White Fleet*, February 22, 1909

Keystone View Company, *President Roosevelt and President-elect Taft Enter the Capitol to Take the Oath of Office*, March 4, 1909

Roosevelt's final public responsibility as president was attendance at Taft's inauguration. On March 4, amid a blizzard, he arrived at the Capitol to participate in his successor's swearing-in. Given the snow, officials decided to hold the ceremony indoors rather than on the steps at the east entrance, the traditional venue for presidential inaugurations. While much attention was paid to the new president, many people could not help but reflect on the outgoing occupant of the White House. Letters poured in to thank him for his service and to wish him well as a private citizen. Journalists wrote in mostly glowing terms about his tenure, with many speculating about his future. Would he return to politics upon his return, as many suspected, or settle into quieter pursuits? Perhaps, as some commented with wry humor, the African lions would render such questions moot. Roosevelt also received at this time numerous parting gifts and tokens of good luck for his upcoming trip. Taft gave him a small gold ruler with the words "Goodbye, Good Luck, and a Safe Return" engraved on its side; his "Tennis Cabinet" held a farewell banquet for him, at which they presented him with a bronze sculpture of a cougar by the artist Alexander P. Proctor; and former heavyweight boxing champion John L. Sullivan gave him a gold-mounted rabbit's foot, which he would carry with him throughout the trip.

Though presidential inaugurations are ostensibly about new beginnings, an idea that Roosevelt honored by departing from Washington for his Long Island home not long after the ceremony, Taft marked the occasion by authoring a glowing tribute entitled "My Predecessor" that ran in *Collier's Weekly* and several other publications on the day of the inauguration. Celebrating Roosevelt's belief "in practical progress and not in ideals which make for no real advancement," Taft wrote that "the relation between Mr. Roosevelt and myself has been one of close and sweet intimacy. It has never been ruffled in the slightest degree, and I do not think that we have ever misunderstood each other." He highlighted many of Roosevelt's achievements as president and then continued by describing his fondness for the outdoors: "He loves the woods; he loves hunting; he loves life akin to that of the pioneer; he loves roughing it," adding, "I don't." With a closing flourish, Taft spoke about his legacy: "When the friction of the last few months shall be forgotten, when the mists of momentary irritation shall have disappeared, the greatness of Theodore Roosevelt as President and leader of men in one of the great moral movements of the country's history will become clearer to everyone, and he will take his place in history with Washington and Lincoln." While the outgoing president appreciated such generous words, the good feelings shared by these two men would not last. Despite taking his leave and immersing himself in his African expedition, Roosevelt could not resist looking in on his successor and at times questioning—most often privately—Taft's actions. Although he professed otherwise, Roosevelt missed the presidency, and feelings of what might have been would color his trip.

On the eve of his departure from New York, *The Outlook* published a short essay by Roosevelt summarizing his intentions. Over the previous three months numerous magazines had written lengthy accounts of his forthcoming trip, none of which he had contributed to or authorized. For the first time Roosevelt wished to speak publicly about the trip's objectives. Titled "A Scientific Expedition," the article emphasized the natural history research on which he and his Smithsonian partners would focus. Rejecting the notion that it was a pleasure trip, he framed it instead as a contribution to knowledge: "It is a scientific expedition. We shall collect birds and mammals for the National Museum at Washington, and nothing will be shot unless for food, or for preservation as a specimen, or unless, of course, the animal is of a noxious kind. There will be no wanton destruction whatever." He closed by asking that no reporters follow him. "If anyone pretends to be with me or pretends to write as to what I do, his statements should be accepted as on their face not merely false but ludicrous. . . . I am a private citizen, and I am entitled to enjoy the privacy that should be the private citizen's right."

On March 23, 1909, three days after the essay's publication, Theodore Roosevelt and his son Kermit left the family home in Oyster Bay and headed by rail to the docks in Hoboken, New Jersey, where the steamer SS *Hamburg* awaited them. Thirty-seven years after his boyhood trip to Egypt, Roosevelt was at last en route back to Africa.

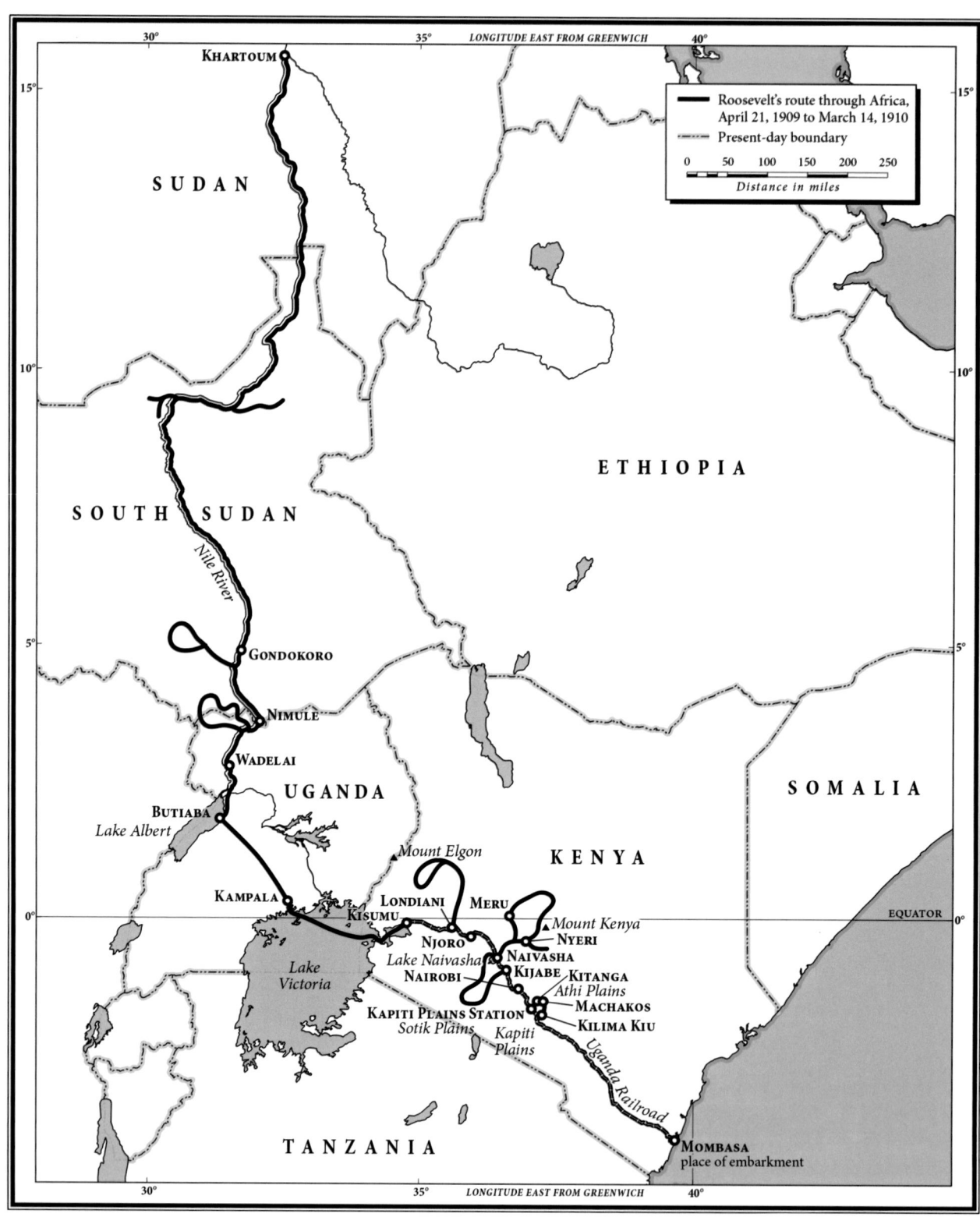

Roosevelt's route through Africa,
April 21, 1909 to March 14, 1910

Present-day boundary

0   50   100   150   200   250

Distance in miles

KHARTOUM

SUDAN

SOUTH SUDAN

Nile River

GONDOKORO

NIMULE

WADELAI

UGANDA

BUTIABA

Lake Albert

KAMPALA

Mount Elgon

KENYA

LONDIANI   MERU

KISUMU

NJORO   *Mount Kenya*

Lake Naivasha   NAIVASHA   NYERI

NAIROBI   KIJABE   KITANGA

Athi Plains

KAPITI PLAINS STATION   MACHAKOS

Sotik Plains   *Kapiti*   KILIMA KIU
          Plains

Uganda Railroad

*Lake
Victoria*

ETHIOPIA

SOMALIA

EQUATOR

TANZANIA

MOMBASA
place of embarkment

THE ROOSEVELT— SMITHSONIAN EXPEDITION

This book features twenty-eight excerpts from *African Game Trails: An Account of the African Wanderings of an American Hunter-Naturalist*. During his year in East Africa, Theodore Roosevelt wrote twelve essays about his travels on commission for the publisher Charles Scribner's Sons. Despite several stretches far removed from transportation and communication hubs, he mailed the essays to his publisher at regular intervals. Beginning in October 1909, *Scribner's Magazine* published one essay each month for the next year. After the expedition's completion, Roosevelt revisited these essays and revised them for publication as a standalone volume. Organized into fifteen chapters with six appendixes, *African Game Trails* was published in September 1910. Given the widespread interest in Roosevelt and the expedition, the book sold well and received much popular and critical notice. While he and others would write again about the expedition in later publications, Roosevelt regarded this book as its definitive record.

An important feature of the essays in *Scribner's Magazine* and *African Game Trails* was the addition of photographic reproductions that accompanied the written text. While Kermit Roosevelt served as the expedition's primary photographer, other members, including naturalists Edmund Heller and J. Alden Loring, also brought cameras to document the places where they traveled, the people they met, and the wildlife they encountered and often killed. Seen together, the resulting collection of more than a thousand photographs represents one of the earliest and most extensive photographic records of East Africa and one of the first to document a major safari in that region. Eighty-eight of these photographs were ultimately selected for publication in *African Game Trails*. Because the cameras they carried were limited in their ability to capture the action of the hunt, the American wildlife illustrator Philip R. Goodwin was recruited to create drawings of dramatic episodes featured in Roosevelt's account. Eight of these drawings were also published.

Kermit Roosevelt's photographs, together with an assortment of other photographs collected during the expedition, are now housed within the Theodore Roosevelt Collection at

Map of the Roosevelt–Smithsonian Expedition in British East Africa, April 21, 1909, to March 14, 1910

Book cover, *African Game Trails*, 1910   Title page, *African Game Trails*, 1910

Harvard University in Cambridge, Massachusetts. This collection documents all elements of the trip from the Roosevelts' departure in March 1909 to their arrival home in June 1910. The Smithsonian Institution Archives in Washington, DC, houses the photographs taken by the naturalists who accompanied the expedition and prepared the natural history specimens for shipment to the United States.

In the pages that follow, a short explanatory account introduces and contextualizes each of the twenty-eight excerpts. In addition, I have selected noteworthy photographs from the expedition to include with related episodes from *African Game Trails*. If known, the author of each photograph is credited. Many of the photographs were not originally titled. As such, the titles are drawn from either notes on the image's verso or a title used in *Scribner's Magazine* or *African Game Trails*.

Roosevelt's Foreword: Looking Back at the Safari's End

Roosevelt dated the foreword to *African Game Trails* March 15, 1910, a day after the expedition reached Khartoum, Sudan. There, eleven months after first landing in Africa, he parted from the remaining members of the safari and reunited with his wife, Edith, and daughter Ethel. Although it would be another three months until he was back home in America, he considered Khartoum the conclusion of the expedition.

Looking back on the preceding eleven months from Khartoum, he wrote about East Africa with great enthusiasm. The abundance of animals and the beauty and variety of the landscape made it the ultimate destination for an elite hunter. It is clear, however, that his ideas about Africa had changed little during the course of the trip. His understanding of the continent prior to his journey was informed directly by the British hunters with whom he had corresponded, European travelogues and popular fiction—especially Rudyard Kipling—and conversations with a small group of American naturalists. These and other, more indirect sources about Africa that prevailed in the West shaped how Roosevelt saw this place and its future.

Roosevelt's ideas about its people also remained little changed. While he acknowledged cultural variation among different African communities, he subscribed to the prevailing belief in Social Darwinism and understood Black Africans more generally as an inferior race belonging to an earlier era in human development.

01   March 15, 1910

"I speak of Africa and golden joys"; the joy of wandering through lonely lands; the joy of hunting the mighty and terrible lords of the wilderness, the cunning, the wary, and the grim. In these greatest of the world's great hunting-grounds there are mountain peaks whose snows are dazzling under the equatorial sun; swamps where the slime oozes and bubbles and festers in the steaming heat; lakes like seas; skies that burn above deserts where the iron desolation is shrouded from view by the wavering mockery of the mirage; vast grassy plains where palms and thorn-trees fringe the dwindling streams; mighty rivers rushing out of the heart of the continent through the sadness of endless marshes; forests of gorgeous beauty, where death broods in the dark and silent depths.

There are regions as healthy as the northland; and other regions, radiant with bright-hued flowers, birds and butterflies, odorous with sweet and heavy scents, but, treacherous in their beauty, and sinister to human life. On the land and in the water there are dread brutes that feed on the flesh of man; and among the lower things, that crawl, and fly, and sting, and bite, he finds swarming foes far more evil and deadly than any beast or reptile; foes that kill his crops and his cattle, foes before which he himself perishes in his hundreds of thousands.

The dark-skinned races that live in the land vary widely. Some are warlike, cattle-owning nomads; some till the soil and live in thatched huts shaped like beehives; some are fisherfolk; some are ape-like naked savages, who dwell in the woods and prey on creatures not much wilder or lower than themselves.

The land teems with beasts of the chase, infinite in number and incredible in variety. It holds the fiercest beasts of ravin, and the fleetest and most timid of those beings that live in undying fear of talon and fang. It holds the largest and the smallest of hoofed animals. It holds the mightiest creatures that tread the earth or swim in its rivers; it also holds distant kinsfolk of these same creatures, no bigger than woodchucks, which dwell in crannies of the rocks, and in the treetops. There are antelope smaller than hares, and antelope larger than oxen. There are creatures which are the embodiments of grace; and others whose huge ungainliness is like that of a shape in a nightmare. The plains are alive with droves of strange and beautiful animals whose like is not known elsewhere; and with others even stranger that show both in form and temper something of the fantastic and the grotesque. It is a never-ending pleasure to gaze at the great herds of buck as they move to and fro in their myriads; as they stand for their noontide rest in the quivering heat haze; as the long files come down to drink at the watering-places; as they feed and fight and rest and make love.

The hunter who wanders through these lands sees sights which ever afterward remain fixed in his mind. He sees the monstrous river-horse snorting and plunging beside the boat; the giraffe looking over the treetops at the nearing horseman; the ostrich fleeing at a speed that none may rival; the snarling leopard and coiled python, with their lethal beauty; the zebras, barking in the moonlight, as the laden caravan passes on its night march through a thirsty land. In after years there shall come to him memories of the lion's charge; of the gray bulk of the elephant, close at hand in the sombre woodland; of the buffalo, his sullen eyes lowering from under his helmet of horn; of the rhinoceros, truculent and stupid, standing in the bright sunlight on the empty plain.

These things can be told. But there are no words that can tell the hidden spirit of the wilderness, that can reveal its mystery, its melancholy, and its charm. There is delight in the hardy life of the open, in long rides rifle in hand, in the thrill of the fight with dangerous game. Apart from this, yet mingled with it is the strong attraction of the silent places, of the large tropic moons, and the splendor of the new stars; where the wanderer sees the awful glory of sunrise and sunset in the wide waste spaces of the earth, unworn of man, and changed only by the slow change of the ages through time everlasting.

Unidentified photographer, *Theodore Roosevelt and the Safari Group with an American Flag*, August 1909

From America to East Africa

Roosevelt's journey bore all the pomp accorded a head of state. From the time he and Kermit left their Long Island home to their arrival in East Africa four weeks later, the ex-president was besieged by the press and swarmed by the public. Departing from New York harbor following a twenty-one-gun salute, the Roosevelts were joined aboard the SS *Hamburg* by the three Smithsonian naturalists and a coterie of unrelated passengers who vied for their attention.

The ship made initial stops in the Azores and Gibraltar. At Naples, Italy, British hunter and expedition advisor Frederick Selous and Francis W. Dawson, the United Press wire service chief in Paris, joined the party. Roosevelt cautioned Dawson that he could travel with them as far as Mombasa, if he promised to turn back there and not to request any interviews. In Naples they boarded the SS *Admiral* and traveled next to Messina to meet King Victor Emmanuel III and to survey the devastating earthquake damage suffered the previous December by that Sicilian city. Witnessing this disaster prompted Roosevelt to write officials in Washington encouraging them to send American supply ships then in Suez to assist in the relief effort.

From there the party steamed east across the Mediterranean to Port Said, Egypt, where the *Admiral* passed through the Suez Canal to the Red Sea. After one final stop at Aden, they turned south toward their destination, Mombasa, on the coast of the British East Africa Protectorate. (Established as a protectorate in 1895, the region was called the Colony of Kenya after 1920 and gained independence from Great Britain in 1963.) Despite several bouts of seasickness, the Roosevelts traveled in comfort and enjoyed the company of their new companions and the authors in the Pigskin Library.

In chapter 1, titled "A Railroad through the Pleistocene," the former president recalls earlier travelers in Africa, including Ptolemy, the second-century Egyptian geographer of Greek descent, as well as nineteenth-century British explorers John Speke, James Grant, and Samuel Baker. In referring to them, he aligned his own expedition as a continuation of this tradition of exploration in Africa.

02 March 23 to April 20, 1909

The great world movement which began with the voyages of Columbus and Vasco da Gama, and which has gone on with ever-increasing rapidity and complexity until our own time, has developed along a myriad lines of interest. In no way has it been more interesting than in the way in which it has brought into sudden, violent, and intimate contact phases of the world's life history which would normally be separated by untold centuries of slow development. Again and again, in the continents new to peoples of European stock, we have seen the spectacle of a high civilization all at once thrust into and superimposed upon a wilderness of savage men and savage beasts. Nowhere, and at no time, has the contrast been more strange and more striking than in British East Africa during the last dozen years.

The country lies directly under the equator; and the hinterland, due west, contains the huge Nyanza lakes, vast inland seas which gather the headwaters of the White Nile. This hinterland, with its lakes and its marshes, its snowcapped mountains, its high, dry plateaus, and its forests of deadly luxuriance, was utterly unknown to white men half a century ago. The map of Ptolemy in the second century of our era gave a more accurate view of the lakes, mountains, and headwaters of the Nile than the maps published at the beginning of the second half of the nineteenth century, just before Speke, Grant, and Baker made their great trips of exploration and adventure. Behind these explorers came others; and then adventurous missionaries, traders, and elephant hunters; and many men, whom risk did not daunt, who feared neither danger nor hardship, traversed the country hither and thither, now for one reason, now for another, now as naturalists, now as geographers, and again as government officials or as mere wanderers who loved the wild and strange life which had survived over from an elder age. . . .

This region, this great fragment out of the long-buried past of our race, is now accessible by railroad to all who care to go thither; and no field more inviting offers itself to hunter or naturalist, while even to the ordinary traveler it teems with interest. On March 23, 1909, I sailed thither from New York, in charge of a scientific expedition sent out by the Smithsonian, to collect birds, mammals, reptiles, and plants, but especially specimens of big game, for the National Museum at Washington. In addition to myself and my son Kermit (who had entered Harvard a few months previously), the party consisted of three naturalists: Surgeon-Lieut. Col. Edgar A. Mearns, USA., retired; Mr. Edmund Heller, of California; and Mr. J. Alden Loring, of Owego, N. Y. My arrangements for the trip had been chiefly made through two valued English friends,

Mr. Frederick Courteney Selous, the greatest of the world's big-game hunters, and Mr. Edward North Buxton, also a mighty hunter. On landing we were to be met by Messrs. R. J. Cuninghame and Leslie Tarlton, both famous hunters; the latter an Australian, who served through the South African war; the former by birth a Scotchman, and a Cambridge man, but long a resident of Africa, and at one time a professional elephant hunter—in addition to having been a whaler in the Arctic Ocean, a hunter-naturalist in Lapland, a transport rider in South Africa, and a collector for the British Museum in various odd corners of the earth.

We sailed on the *Hamburg* from New York—what headway the Germans have made among those who go down to the sea in ships!—and at Naples trans-shipped to the *Admiral*, of another German line, the East African. On both ships we were as comfortable as possible, and the voyage was wholly devoid of incidents. Now and then, as at the Azores, at Suez, and at Aden, the three naturalists landed, and collected some dozens or scores of birds—which next day were skinned and prepared in my room, as the largest and best fitted for the purpose.

Unidentified photographer, *Theodore Roosevelt Inspects Crates of Ammunition*, March 23, 1909

Left: Unidentified photographer, *Theodore Roosevelt's Safari Equipment, Hoboken, New Jersey*, March 23, 1909

Next page: Brown Brothers, *Mr. Roosevelt off for Africa on the* Hamburg, March 23, 1909

Paul Thompson, *Theodore Roosevelt at Naples; Minister Lloyd Griscom behind with Silk Hat*, April 5, 1909

After reaching Suez the ordinary tourist type of passenger ceased to be predominant; in his place there were Italian officers going out to a desolate coast town on the edge of Somaliland; missionaries, German, English, and American; Portuguese civil officials; traders of different nationalities; and planters and military and civil officers bound to German and British East Africa. The Englishmen included planters, magistrates, forest officials, army officers on leave from India, and other army officers going out to take command of black native levies in out-of-the-way regions where the English flag stands for all that makes life worth living. They were a fine set, these young Englishmen, whether dashing army officers or capable civilians; they reminded me of our own men who have reflected such honor on the American name, whether in civil and military positions in the Philippines and Puerto Rico, working on the Canal Zone in Panama, taking care of the customhouses in San Domingo, or serving in the army of occupation in Cuba. Moreover, I felt as if I knew most of them already, for they might have walked out of the pages of Kipling. But I was not as well prepared for the corresponding and

Unidentified photographer, *Theodore Roosevelt, Frederick Selous, Edgar A. Mearns, and Kermit Roosevelt aboard the SS* Admiral, April 1909

equally interesting types among the Germans, the planters, the civil officials, the officers who had commanded, or were about to command, white or native troops; men of evident power and energy, seeing whom made it easy to understand why German East Africa has thriven apace. They are first-class men, these English and Germans; both are doing in East Africa a work of worth to the whole world; there is ample room for both, and no possible cause for any but a thoroughly friendly rivalry; and it is earnestly to be wished, in the interest both of them and of outsiders, too, that their relations will grow, as they ought to grow, steadily better—and not only in East Africa but everywhere else.

Next page: Unidentified photographer, *Kermit Roosevelt Shops on a Street in Ismailia, Egypt*, April 1909

Arrival in Mombasa

The SS *Admiral* arrived at the port of Mombasa in the late afternoon of April 21, 1909. Crowds gathered to see the former American president, but it was dark by the time Roosevelt and his entourage came ashore. Many awaited his visit with excitement, especially those British who were themselves relatively new arrivals. Frederick John Jackson, the new acting governor of the protectorate, led the delegation gathered to greet the party. As the party disembarked, however, a sudden rainstorm dampened the welcome. The *East African Standard* reported: "The night was one of the wettest experienced in Mombasa and many who attended were put to considerable personal inconvenience, but so keen was the desire to welcome the ex-President and to do honor to so distinguished a guest that not a single chair was vacant."

That evening Jackson hosted a dinner at the Mombasa Club, where he read a telegram from King Edward VII welcoming the Roosevelts. Others spoke, including Frederick Selous, who encouraged the former president to assist in furthering diplomatic relations between England and Germany, both nations having recently established colonial outposts in the region. Roosevelt also spoke and praised the British efforts in Africa.

Although Roosevelt had previously decided that no journalists would join the safari, British filmmaker Cherry Kearton—author, with his brother Richard, of the first book-length portfolio of wild animal photography ever to be published—was present in Mombasa and created footage of Roosevelt's time there. American naturalist James L. Clark had recruited Kearton to accompany an East African expedition organized by the American Museum of Natural History. Their paths would cross at various points over the next six months, and the resulting footage became the film *Roosevelt in Africa*, which premiered in the United States in April 1910.

In describing his arrival in Mombasa, Roosevelt foregrounded the region's long history of trade and colonial occupation by different groups. In doing so, he left unmentioned the Indigenous African population and their long-standing rivalry with these outsiders, thereby perpetuating the misconception that East Africa was a largely "barren" land.

03 April 21, 1909

There were on the ship many men who loved wild nature, and who were keen hunters of big game; and almost every day, as we steamed over the hot, smooth waters of the Red Sea and the Indian Ocean, we would gather on deck around Selous to listen to tales of those strange adventures that only come to the man who has lived long the lonely life of the wilderness.

Edmund Heller, *Baobab Tree, Streets of Mombasa*, April 22, 1909

On April 21 we steamed into the beautiful and picturesque harbor of Mombasa. Many centuries before the Christian era, dhows from Arabia, carrying seafarers of Semitic races whose very names have perished, rounded the Lion's Head at Guardafui and crept slowly southward along the barren African coast. Such dhows exist today almost unchanged, and bold indeed were the men who first steered them across the unknown oceans. They were men of iron heart and supple conscience, who fronted inconceivable danger and hardship; they established trading stations for gold and ivory and slaves; they turned these trading stations into little cities and sultanates, half Arab, half negro. Mombasa was among them. In her time of brief splendor Portugal seized the city; the Arabs won it back; and now England holds it. It lies just south of the equator, and when we saw it the brilliant green of the tropic foliage showed the town at its best.

We were welcomed to Government House in most cordial fashion by the acting Governor, Lieutenant-Governor Jackson, who is not only a trained public official of long experience but a first-class field naturalist and a renowned big-game hunter; indeed I could not too warmly express my appreciation of the hearty and generous courtesy with which we were received and treated alike by the official and the unofficial world throughout East Africa. We landed in the kind of torrential downpour that only comes in the tropics; it reminded me of Panama at certain moments in the rainy season. That night we were given a dinner by the Mombasa Club; and it was interesting to meet the merchants and planters of the town and the neighborhood as well as the officials.

The Uganda Railway

Roosevelt was not in Mombasa long, for he was eager to begin the safari. Less than twenty-four hours after his arrival, the party, including Frederick John Jackson, acting governor of the British East Africa Protectorate, boarded the governor's private rail car and began a 275-mile train journey inland to the Kapiti Plains Station. They stopped in the village of Samburu for the night and arrived at their destination the following afternoon.

Mombasa served as the eastern terminus of the Uganda Railway, an ambitious project that the British began in 1896 to connect the coast with Uganda's Lake Victoria, one of the sources of the Nile River. Known colloquially as the "lunatic line" by British politicians who opposed its construction and the "iron snake" by local Kikuyu tribespeople, the railroad required the work of more than 32,000 laborers imported from India and took five years to complete. Given difficult conditions, nearly 2,500 of them died during its construction. Yet, to those who believed in British colonialism, the line promised to open the East African interior to European farmers, traders, missionaries, and tourists. Likening the territory to the American West, the former president hoped that Americans would join others in settling and developing this region.

During the trip the Roosevelts enjoyed the scenery and commented upon a host of subjects, including the importance of game reserves to manage wildlife.

 **04**　**April 22 and 23, 1909**

The day after we landed we boarded the train to take what seems to me, as I think it would to most men fond of natural history, the most interesting railway journey in the world. It was Governor Jackson's special train, and in addition to his own party and ours there was only Selous; and we travelled with the utmost comfort through a naturalist's wonderland. All civilized governments are now realizing that it is their duty here and there to preserve, unharmed, tracts of wild nature, with thereon the wild things the destruction of which means the destruction of half the charm of wild nature. The English Government has made a large game reserve of much of the region on the way to Nairobi, stretching far to the south, and one mile to the north, of the track. The reserve swarms with game; it would be of little value except as a reserve; and the attraction it now offers to travelers renders it an asset of real consequence to the whole colony. The wise people of Maine, in our own country, have discovered that

Unidentified photographer, *Theodore Roosevelt Arrives at Mombasa Station*, April 22, 1909

intelligent game preservation, carried out in good faith, and in a spirit of common-sense as far removed from mushy sentimentality as from brutality, results in adding one more to the State's natural resources of value; and in consequence there are more moose and deer in Maine today than there were forty years ago; there is a better chance for every man in Maine, rich or poor, provided that he is not a game butcher, to enjoy his share of good hunting; and the number of sportsmen and tourists attracted to the State adds very appreciably to the means of livelihood of the citizen. Game reserves should not be established where they are detrimental to the interests of large bodies of settlers, nor yet should they be nominally established in regions so remote that the only men really interfered with are those who respect the law, while a premium is thereby put on the activity of the unscrupulous persons who are eager to break it. Similarly, game laws should be drawn primarily in the interest of the whole people, keeping steadily in mind certain facts that ought to be self-evident to everyone above the intellectual level of those well-meaning persons who apparently think that all shooting is wrong and that man could continue to exist if all wild animals were allowed to increase unchecked. There must be recognition of the fact that almost any wild animal of the defenseless type, if its multiplication were unchecked while its natural enemies, the dangerous carnivores, were killed, would by its simple increase crowd man off the planet; and of the further fact that, far short of such increase, a time speedily comes when the existence of too much game is incompatible with the interests, or indeed existence, of the cultivator. As in most other matters, it is only the happy mean which is healthy and rational. There should be certain sanctuaries and nurseries where game can live and breed absolutely unmolested; and elsewhere the laws should so far as possible provide for the continued existence of the game in sufficient numbers to allow a reasonable amount of hunting on fair terms to any hardy and vigorous man fond of the sport, and yet not in sufficient numbers to jeopardize the interests of the actual settler, the tiller of the soil, the man whose well-being should be the prime object to be kept in mind by every statesman. Game butchery is as objectionable as any other form of wanton cruelty or barbarity; but to protest against all hunting of game is a sign of softness of head, not of soundness of heart. . . .

Next morning we were in the game country, and as we sat on the seat over the cow-catcher it was literally like passing through a vast zoological garden. Indeed no such railway journey can be taken on any other line in any other land. At one time we passed a herd of a dozen or so of great giraffes, cows and calves, cantering along through the open woods a couple of hundred yards to the right of the train. Again, still closer, four waterbuck cows, their big ears thrown forward, stared at us without moving until we had passed. Hartebeests were everywhere; one herd was on the track, and when the engine whistled they bucked and sprang with ungainly agility and galloped clear of the danger. A long-tailed straw-colored monkey ran from one tree to another. Huge black ostriches appeared from time to time. Once a troop of impala, close by the track, took fright; and as the beautiful creatures fled we saw now one and now another bound clear over the high bushes. A herd of zebra clattered across a cutting of the line not a hundred yards ahead of the train; the whistle hurried their progress, but only for a moment, and as we passed they were already turning round to gaze. The wild creatures were in their sanctuary, and they knew it. Some of the settlers have at times grumbled at this game reserve being kept of such size; but surely it is one of the most valuable possessions the country could have. The lack of water in parts, the prevalence in other parts of diseases harmful to both

Unidentified photographer, *Mr. Roosevelt, Governor Jackson, Mr. Selous, and Dr. Mearns in Front of the Engine on the Way to Kapiti*, April 22, 1909

Kermit Roosevelt, *Hartebeests*, April or May 1909

civilized man and domestic cattle, render this great tract of country the home of all homes for the creatures of the waste. The protection given these wild creatures is genuine, not nominal; they are preserved, not for the pleasure of the few, but for the good of all who choose to see this strange and attractive spectacle; and from this nursery and breeding-ground the overflow keeps up the stock of game in the adjacent land, to the benefit of the settler to whom the game gives fresh meat, and to the benefit of the whole country because of the attraction it furnishes to all who desire to visit a veritable happy hunting ground.

Hunting on the Kapiti and Athi Plains

Upon arriving at the Kapiti Plains Station, about forty miles southeast of the capital city, Nairobi, Roosevelt and his party were greeted by representatives from the safari outfitter Newland, Tarlton & Company and the Africans who had been recruited to accompany the expedition. Most were Swahili men who lived near the coast. Gathered in military formation, some two hundred porters stood at the ready to shoulder the needed equipment and supplies, including sixty barrels of salt for the preservation of the animal specimens they hoped to collect. There Roosevelt met the gun bearers, horse tenders, trackers, and camp orderlies who would provide for his safety and comfort and would assist with the hunt. Seventy-three tents had been erected in neat rows, with a large American flag flying over the former president's.

Sir Alfred Pease, a former member of the British Parliament, who owned a seven-thousand-acre ostrich ranch on the nearby Athi Plains, was also there to welcome the Roosevelts. For the next two weeks, he served as their de facto host, assisting the safari as it got underway. After three days spent sorting out their equipment and getting settled in camp, hunting began at last.

05 April 23 to May 11, 1909

Soon after lunch we drew up at the little station of Kapiti Plains, where our safari was awaiting us; "safari" being the term employed throughout East Africa to denote both the caravan with which one makes an expedition and the expedition itself. Our aim being to cure and send home specimens of all the common big game—in addition to as large a series as possible of the small mammals and birds—it was necessary to carry an elaborate apparatus of naturalists' supplies; we had brought with us, for instance, four tons of fine salt, as to cure the skins of the big beasts is a herculean labor under the best conditions; we had hundreds of traps for the small creatures; many boxes of shot-gun cartridges in addition to the ordinary rifle cartridges which alone would be necessary on a hunting trip; and, in short, all the many impedimenta needed if scientific work is to be properly done under modern conditions. Few laymen have any idea of the expense and pains which must be undergone in order to provide groups of mounted big animals from far-off lands, such as we see in museums like the National Museum in Washington and the American Museum of Natural History in New York. The modern naturalist must realize

Unidentified photographer, *Theodore Roosevelt Expedition Train at Kapiti Station*, April 23, 1909

that in some of its branches his profession, while more than ever a science, has also become an art. So our preparations were necessarily on a very large scale; and as we drew up at the station the array of porters and of tents looked as if some small military expedition was about to start. As a compliment, which I much appreciated, a large American flag was floating over my own tent; and in the front line, flanking this tent on either hand, were other big tents for the members of the party, with a dining tent and skinning tent; while behind were the tents of the two hundred porters, the gun-bearers, the tent boys, the askaris or native soldiers, and the horse boys or saises. In front of the tents stood the men in two lines; the first containing the fifteen askaris, the second the porters with their headmen. The askaris were uniformed, each in a red fez, a blue blouse, and white knickerbockers, and each carrying his rifle and belt. The porters were chosen from several different tribes or races to minimize the danger of combination in the event of mutiny. . . .

Equatorial Africa is in most places none too healthy a place for the white man, and he must care for himself as he would scorn to do in the lands of pine and birch and frosty weather. Camping in the Rockies or the North Woods can with advantage be combined with

Edmund Heller, *The Askaris and Porters Drawn Up in a Line to Greet Us*, April 1909

"roughing it"; and the early pioneers of the West, the explorers, prospectors, and hunters, who always roughed it, were as hardy as bears, and lived to a hale old age, if Indians and accidents permitted. But in tropic Africa a lamentable proportion of the early explorers paid in health or life for the hardships they endured; and throughout most of the country no man can long rough it, in the Western and Northern sense, with impunity.

At Kapiti Plains our tents, our accommodations generally, seemed almost too comfortable for men who knew camp life only on the Great Plains, in the Rockies, and in the North Woods. My tent had a fly which was to protect it from the great heat; there was a little rear extension in which I bathed—a hot bath, never a cold bath, is almost a tropic necessity; there was a ground canvas, of vital moment in a land of ticks, jiggers, and scorpions; and a cot to sleep on, so as to be raised from the ground. Quite a contrast to life on the round-up! Then I had two tent boys to see after my belongings, and to wait at table as well as in the tent. Ali, a Mohammedan mulatto (Arab and negro), was the chief of the two, and spoke some English, while under him was "Bill," a speechless black boy; Ali being particularly faithful and efficient. Two other Mohammedan negroes, clad like the askaris, reported to me as my gun-bearers, Muhamed and Bakari;

Kermit Roosevelt, *Theodore Roosevelt Stands in Front of a Line of African Men*, April 1909

seemingly excellent men, loyal and enduring, no trackers, but with keen eyes for game, and the former speaking a little English. My two horse boys, or saises, were both pagans. One, Hamisi, must have had in his veins Galla or other non-negro blood; derived from the Hamitic, or bastard Semitic, or at least non-negro, tribes which, pushing slowly and fitfully southward and south-westward among the negro peoples, have created an intricate tangle of ethnic and linguistic types from the middle Nile to far south of the equator. Hamisi always wore a long feather in one of his sandals, the only ornament he affected. The other sais was a silent, gentle-mannered black heathen; his name was Simba, a lion, and as I shall later show he was not unworthy of it. The two horses for which these men cared were stout, quiet little beasts; one, a sorrel, I named Tranquillity, and the other, a brown, had so much the coblike build of a zebra that we christened him Zebra-shape. One of Kermit's two horses, by the way, was more romantically named after Huandaw, the sharp-eared steed of the Mabinogion. Cuninghame, lean, sinewy, bearded, exactly the type of hunter and safari manager that one would wish for such an expedition as ours, had ridden up with us on the train, and at the station we met Tarlton, and also two settlers of the

Edmund Heller, *Our First Camp, Kapiti Plains Station*, April 1909

neighborhood, Sir Alfred Pease and Mr. Clifford Hill. Hill was an Africander. He and his cousin, Harold Hill, after serving through the South African war, had come to the new country of British East Africa to settle, and they represented the ideal type of settler for taking the lead in the spread of empire. They were descended from the English colonists who came to South Africa in 1820; they had never been in England, and neither had Tarlton. It was exceedingly interesting to meet these Australians and Africanders, who typified in their lives and deeds the greatness of the English Empire, and yet had never seen England.

As for Sir Alfred, Kermit and I were to be his guests for the next fortnight, and we owe primarily to him, to his mastery of hunting craft, and his unvarying and generous hospitality and kindness, the pleasure and success of our introduction to African hunting. His life had been one of such varied interest as has only been possible in our own generation. He had served many years in Parliament; he had for some years been a magistrate in a peculiarly responsible post in the Transvaal; he had journeyed and hunted and explored in the northern Sahara, in the Soudan, in Somaliland, in Abyssinia; and now he was ranching in East Africa. A singularly good rider and one of the best game shots I have ever seen, it would have been impossible to have found a kinder host or a hunter better fitted to teach us how to begin our work with African big game.

Trekking in the Wilderness

Roosevelt was curious about all facets of natural history. While much attention in records of the safari focused on his pursuit of large mammals, he was also interested in smaller animals and in other scientific realms such as botany and ornithology. The diversity of East Africa's wilderness fascinated him, and whether riding on horseback or walking on foot, he was attentive to most everything in his midst. With guidance and support from the Smithsonian naturalists, he was also keen to build collections for the National Museum of small mammal, plant, and bird specimens. Of the more than 23,000 natural history specimens collected during the expedition, only about a fifth were mammals. Photographs from the expedition reveal this commitment to documenting and collecting a broad spectrum of animals and plants.

Yet, in *African Game Trails*, Roosevelt was most interested in relating stories about hunting large mammals. Most often he and his party were successful. In telling these tales, he was circumspect about this activity, often reminding readers of the expedition's larger purpose and explaining that the meat was not only consumed but needed by all who were a part of this safari. Such statements suggest that earlier criticism leveled at him about hunting's destructive nature continued to resonate.

06 Late April 1909

The habits of the game as to migration vary with the different districts, in Africa as in America. There are places where all the game, perhaps notably the wildebeests, gather in herds of thousands, at certain times, and travel for scores of miles, so that a district which is teeming with game at one time may be almost barren of large wildlife at another. But my information was that around the Kapiti Plains there was no such complete and extensive shift. If the rains are abundant and the grass rank, most of the game will be found far out in the middle of the plains; if, as was the case at the time of my visit, there has been a long drought—the game will be found ten or fifteen miles away, near or among the foothills.

Unless there was something special on, like a lion or rhinoceros hunt, I usually rode off followed only by my sais and gun-bearers. I cannot describe the beauty and the unceasing

Kermit Roosevelt, *Father with a Papyrus Stalk, Showing Height to which Papyrus Often Attained in the Swamp*, 1909

76

Edmund Heller, *Tree with Wakamba Beehives, Kitanga*, May 1909

interest of these rides, through the teeming herds of game. It was like retracing the steps of time for sixty or seventy years and being back in the days of Cornwallis Harris and Gordon Cumming, in the palmy times of the giant fauna of South Africa. On Pease's own farm one day I passed through scores of herds of the beautiful and wonderful wild creatures I have spoken of above; all told there were several thousands of them. With the exception of the wildebeest, most of them were not shy, and I could have taken scores of shots at a distance of a couple of hundred yards or thereabout. Of course, I did not shoot at anything unless we were out of meat or needed the skin for the collection; and when we took the skin we almost always took the meat too, for the porters, although they had their rations of rice, depended for much of their well-being on our success with the rifle.

Edmund Heller, *Giant Lobelia*, 1909

These rides through the wild, lonely country, with only my silent black followers, had a peculiar charm. When the sky was overcast it was cool and pleasant, for it is a high country; as soon as the sun appeared the vertical tropic rays made the air quiver above the scorched land. As we passed down a hillside we brushed through aromatic shrubs and the hot pleasant fragrance enveloped us. When we came to a nearly dry watercourse, there would be beds of rushes, beautiful lilies and lush green plants with staring flowers; and great deep-green fig-trees, or flat-topped mimosas. In many of these trees there were sure to be native beehives; these were sections of hollow logs hung from the branches; they formed striking and characteristic features of the landscape. Wherever there was any moisture there were flowers, brilliant of hue and many of them sweet of smell; and birds of numerous kinds abounded. When we left the hills and the wooded watercourses we might ride hour after hour across the barren desolation of the flats, while herds of zebra and hartebeest stared at us through the heat haze. Then the zebra, with shrill, barking neighs, would file off across the horizon, or the high-withered hartebeests, snorting and bucking, would rush off in a confused mass, as unreasoning panic succeeded foolish confidence. If I shot anything, vultures of several kinds, and the tall, hideous marabout storks, gathered before the skinners were through with their work; they usually stayed at a wary distance, but the handsome ravens, glossy-hued with white napes, big-billed, long-winged, and short-tailed, came round more familiarly.

Hunting Lions with Sir Albert Pease

Sir Albert Pease typified the British individuals who were settling East Africa during the first decade of the twentieth century. Educated at Trinity College, Cambridge, he began his career as a banker and a politician. A passion for hunting led him initially to South Africa, but in 1906, after a period of ill health and financial reversals, he decided to search for a new home in East Africa. He settled on prairie land southeast of Nairobi and close to the lines of the Uganda Railway. A founding member of the Shikar Club, a sporting organization in London devoted to big-game hunting, he was a leading figure in the circle of white East African hunters.

For the former president, Pease's reputation and the ranch's close proximity to the railroad made a visit there an obvious choice. For three days after their arrival at the Kapiti Plains Station, the Roosevelts participated in short hunting trips amid intermittent rain. On April 27, eager to score their first major kill, they ventured out to search for a lion. Pease accompanied them, as well as his wife Helen, his daughter Lavender, his future son-in-law Walter Sandfield Medlicott, the white hunting guide Philip Percival, and several unidentified African attendants. They failed to find a lion that day but continued their pursuit. Two days later they succeeded.

 **April 27 to April 29, 1909**

After lunch we began to beat down a long donga, or dry watercourse—a creek, as we should call it in the Western plains country. The watercourse, with low, steep banks, wound in curves, and here and there were patches of brush, which might contain anything in the shape of lion, cheetah, hyena, or wild dog. Soon we came upon lion spoor in the sandy bed; first the footprints of a big male, then those of a lioness. We walked cautiously along each side of the donga, the horses following close behind so that if the lion were missed, we could gallop after him and round him up on the plain. The dogs—for besides the little bull, we had a large brindled mongrel named Ben, whose courage belied his looks—began to show signs of scenting the lion; and we beat out each patch of brush, the natives shouting and throwing in stones, while we stood with the rifles where we could best command any probable exit. After a couple of false alarms, the dogs drew toward one patch, their hair bristling, and showing

Next page: Kermit Roosevelt, *Start of the First Day's Lion Hunt*, April 27, 1909

81

Helen Fowler Pease, *View of the Rock Where We Lunched the Day We Got the First Four Lions*, April 29, 1909

such eager excitement that it was evident something big was inside; and in a moment one of the boys called, "simba" (lion), and pointed with his finger. It was just across the little ravine, there about four yards wide and as many feet deep; and I shifted my position, peering eagerly into the bushes for some moments before I caught a glimpse of tawny hide; as it moved, there was a call to me to "shoot," for at that distance, if the lion charged, there would be scant time to stop it; and I fired into what I saw. There was a commotion in the bushes, and Kermit fired; and immediately afterward there broke out on the other side, not the hoped-for big lion, but two cubs the size of mastiffs. Each was badly wounded, and we finished them off; even if unwounded, they were too big to take alive.

This was a great disappointment, and as it was well on in the afternoon, and we had beaten the country most apt to harbor our game, it seemed unlikely that we would have another chance. Percival was on foot and a long way from his house, so he started for it; and the rest of us also began to jog homeward. But Sir Alfred, although he said nothing, intended to have another try. After going a mile or two he started off to the left at a brisk canter; and we, the other riders, followed, leaving behind our gun-bearers, saises, and porters. A couple of miles away was another donga, another shallow watercourse with occasional big brush patches along the winding bed; and toward this we cantered. Almost as soon as we reached it our leader found the spoor of two big lions; and with every sense acock, we dismounted and approached the first patch of tall bushes. We shouted and threw in stones, but nothing came out; and another small patch showed the same result. Then we mounted our horses again and rode toward another patch a quarter of a mile off. I was mounted on Tranquillity, the stout and quiet sorrel.

This patch of tall, thick brush stood on the hither bank—that is, on our side of the watercourse. We rode up to it and shouted loudly. The response was immediate, in the shape of loud gruntings, and crashings through the thick brush. We were off our horses in an instant, I throwing the reins over the head of mine; and without delay the good old fellow began placidly grazing, quite unmoved by the ominous sounds immediately in front.

I sprang to one side; and for a second or two we waited, uncertain whether we should see the lions charging out ten yards distant or running away. Fortunately, they adopted the latter course. Right in front of me, thirty yards off, there appeared, from behind the bushes which had first screened him from my eyes, the tawny, galloping form of a big maneless lion. Crack! the Winchester spoke; and as the soft-nosed bullet ploughed forward through his flank the lion swerved so that I missed him with the second shot; but my third bullet went through the spine and forward into his chest. Down he came, sixty yards off, his hind quarters dragging, his head up, his ears back, his jaws open and lips drawn up in a prodigious snarl, as he endeavored to turn to face us. His back was broken; but of this we could not at the moment be sure, and if it had merely been grazed, he might have recovered, and then, even though dying, his charge might have done mischief. So Kermit, Sir Alfred, and I fired, almost together, into his chest. His head sank, and he died.

This lion had come out on the left of the bushes; the other, to the right of them, had not been hit, and we saw him galloping off across the plain, six or eight hundred yards away. A couple more shots missed, and we mounted our horses to try to ride him down. The plain sloped gently upward for three-quarters of a mile to a low crest or divide, and long before we got near him, he disappeared over this. Sir Alfred and Kermit were tearing along in front and to the right, with Miss Pease close behind; while Tranquillity carried me, as fast as he could, on the left, with

Medlicott near me. On topping the divide Sir Alfred and Kermit missed the lion, which had swung to the left, and they raced ahead too far to the right. Medlicott and I, however, saw the lion, loping along close behind some kongoni; and this enabled me to get up to him as quickly as the lighter men on the faster horses. The going was now slightly downhill, and the sorrel took me along very well, while Medlicott, whose horse was slow, bore to the right and joined the other two men. We gained rapidly, and, finding out this, the lion suddenly halted and came to bay in a slight hollow, where the grass was rather long. The plain seemed flat, and we could see the lion well from horseback; but, especially when he lay down, it was most difficult to make him out on foot, and impossible to do so when kneeling.

We were about a hundred and fifty yards from the lion, Sir Alfred, Kermit, Medlicott, and Miss Pease off to one side, and slightly above him on the slope, while I was on the level, about equidistant from him and them. Kermit and I tried shooting from the horses; but at such a distance this was not effective. Then Kermit got off, but his horse would not let him shoot; and when I got off, I could not make out the animal through the grass with sufficient distinctness to enable me to take aim. Old Ben the dog had arrived, and, barking loudly, was strolling about near the lion, which paid him not the slightest attention. At this moment my black sais, Simba, came running up to me and took hold of the bridle; he had seen the chase from the line of march and had cut across to join me. . . .

I was still unable to see the lion when I knelt, but he was now standing up, looking first at one group of horses and then at the other, his tail lashing to and fro, his head held low, and his lips dropped over his mouth in peculiar fashion, while his harsh and savage growling rolled thunderously over the plain. Seeing Simba and me on foot, he turned toward us, his tail lashing quicker and quicker. Resting my elbow on Simba's bent shoulder, I took steady aim and pressed the trigger; the bullet went in between the neck and shoulder, and the lion fell over on his side, one foreleg in the air. He recovered in a moment and stood up, evidently very sick, and once more faced me, growling hoarsely. I think he was on the eve of charging. I fired again at once, and this bullet broke his back just behind the shoulders; and with the next I killed him outright, after we had gathered round him.

These were two good-sized maneless lions; and very proud of them I was. . . . It was late before we got the lions skinned. Then we set off toward the ranch, two porters carrying each lion skin, strapped to a pole; and two others carrying the cub skins. Night fell long before we were near the ranch, but the brilliant tropic moon lighted the trail. The stalwart savages who carried the bloody lion skins swung along at a faster walk as the sun went down and the moon rose higher; and they began to chant in unison, one uttering a single word or sentence, and the

Unidentified photographer, *Kermit Roosevelt, Alfred Pease, and Theodore Roosevelt at the Carcass of the First Big Lion*, April 1909

others joining in a deep-toned, musical chorus. The men on a safari, and indeed African natives generally, are always excited over the death of a lion, and the hunting tribes then chant their rough hunting songs, or victory songs, until the monotonous, rhythmical repetitions make them grow almost frenzied. The ride home through the moonlight, the vast barren landscape shining like silver on either hand, was one to be remembered; and above all, the sight of our trophies and of their wild bearers.

Hunting Giraffes with Captain Arthur Slatter

Three months before his departure, Roosevelt met with filmmaker William Selig at the White House. The founder of the Selig Polyscope Company in Chicago, Selig brought with him a film projector and several movies to show to the president and his family. His hope was to secure an invitation to accompany and film the safari. However, after objections from Smithsonian officials and concerns about possible negative publicity, Roosevelt did not offer him one.

Believing that a cinematic account inspired by the trip had great commercial potential, Selig decided to create a fictional account of the expedition without Roosevelt's permission. With assistance from his friend John Ringling, the filmmaker secured animals and wranglers from a Wisconsin circus, including an old lion he purchased for $300. He recruited a vaudeville actor to play Roosevelt and a group of local African Americans to act as porters and hunting guides. Ten scenes were filmed in a day, including a climactic episode in which Roosevelt shoots and kills the recently acquired lion.

A savvy promoter, Selig delayed the movie's release until the inevitable stories about Roosevelt's hunting success began to be published. While Roosevelt had banned journalists from accompanying the safari—at least initially—reports about noteworthy events did get out and soon circulated widely. Learning the news of his success hunting lions on the Kapiti Plains, Selig released his fake documentary *Hunting Big Game in Africa* on May 20. The movie was an instant success, drawing large crowds and enthusiastic press. A year later, while traveling after the safari in Europe, Roosevelt came upon the film at a Berlin theater. He decided to see it and left outraged that it had been produced.

Meanwhile, hunting continued on the Kapiti and Athi Plains. In early May, Roosevelt partnered with Captain Arthur Slatter for several days of hunting. Like Pease, Slatter was a British settler who operated an ostrich farm in the region. With him, Roosevelt killed his first rhinoceros and encountered a group of giraffes.

 **Early May 1909**

Early next morning I went back to camp, and soon after reaching there again started out for a hunt. In the afternoon I came on giraffes and got up near enough to shoot at them. But they are such enormous beasts that I thought them far nearer than they were. My bullet fell short,

Kermit Roosevelt, *Giraffe at Home*, May 1909

and they disappeared among the mimosas, at their strange leisurely looking gallop. Of all the beasts in an African landscape none is more striking than the giraffe. Usually, it is found in small parties or in herds of fifteen or twenty or more individuals. Although it will drink regularly if occasion offers, it is able to get along without water for months at a time and frequents by choice the dry plains or else the stretches of open forest where the trees are scattered and ordinarily somewhat stunted. Like the rhinoceros—the ordinary or prehensile-lipped rhinoceros—the giraffe is a browsing and not a grazing animal. The leaves, buds, and twigs of the mimosas or thorn-trees form its customary food. Its extraordinary height enables it to bring into play to the best possible advantage its noteworthy powers of vision, and no animal is harder to approach unseen. Again and again, I have made it out a mile off or rather have seen it a mile off when it was pointed out to me, and looking at it through my glasses, would see that it was gazing steadily at us. It is a striking-looking animal and handsome in its way, but its length of leg and neck and sloping back make it appear awkward even at rest. When alarmed it may go off at a long swinging pace or walk, but if really frightened it strikes into a peculiar gallop or canter. The tail is cocked and twisted, and the huge hind legs are thrown forward well to the outside of the forelegs. The movements seem deliberate, and the giraffe does not appear to be going at a fast pace, but if it has any start a horse must gallop hard to overtake it. When it starts on this gait, the neck may be dropped forward at a sharp angle with the straight line of the deep chest, and the big head is thrust in advance. They are defenseless things and, though they may kick at a man who incautiously comes within reach, they are in no way dangerous.

Edmund Heller, *The Old Bull Athi Giraffe and Heller's Wakamba Skinners*, May 1909

The following day I again rode out with Captain Slatter. During the morning, we saw nothing except the ordinary game, and we lunched on a hill-top, ten miles distant from camp, under a huge fig-tree with spreading branches and thick, deep-green foliage. Throughout the time we were taking lunch a herd of zebras watched us from nearby, standing motionless with their ears pricked forward, their beautifully striped bodies showing finely in the sunlight. We scanned the country round about with our glasses, and made out first a herd of elands, a mile in our rear, and then three giraffes a mile and a half in our front. I wanted a bull eland, but I wanted a giraffe still more, and we mounted our horses and rode toward where the three tall beasts stood, on an open hillside with trees thinly scattered over it. Half a mile from them we left the horses in a thick belt of timber beside a dry watercourse and went forward on foot.

There was no use in trying a stalk, for that would merely have aroused the giraffe's suspicion. But we knew they were accustomed to the passing and repassing of Wakamba men and women, whom they did not fear if they kept at a reasonable distance, so we walked in single file diagonally in their direction; that is, toward a tree which I judged to be about three hundred yards from them. I was carrying the Winchester loaded with full metal-patched bullets. I wished to get for the museum both a bull and a cow. One of the three giraffes was much larger than the other two, and as he was evidently a bull I thought the two others were cows.

As we reached the tree the giraffes showed symptoms of uneasiness. One of the smaller ones began to make off, and both the others shifted their positions slightly, curling their tails. I instantly dropped on my knee and getting the bead just behind the big bull's shoulder, I fired with the three-hundred-yard sight. I heard the "pack" of the bullet as it struck just where I aimed; and away went all three giraffes at their queer rocking-horse canter. Running forward I emptied my magazine, firing at the big bull and also at one of his smaller companions, and then, slipping into the barrel what proved to be a soft-nosed bullet, I fired at the latter again. The giraffe was going straightaway, and it was a long shot, at four or five hundred yards; but by good luck the bullet broke its back and down it came. The others were now getting over the crest of the hill, but the big one was evidently sick, and we called and beckoned to the two saises to hurry up with the horses. The moment they arrived we jumped on, and Captain Slatter cantered up a neighboring hill so as to mark the direction in which the giraffes went if I lost sight of them. Meanwhile I rode full speed after the giant quarry. I was on the tranquil sorrel, the horse I much preferred in riding down game of any kind, because he had a fair turn of speed, and yet was good about letting me get on and off. As soon as I reached the hillcrest, I saw the giraffes ahead of me, not as far off as I had feared, and I raced toward them without regard to rotten ground and wart-hog holes. The wounded one lagged behind, but when I got near, he put on a spurt, and as I thought I was close enough I leaped off, throwing the reins over the sorrel's head, and opened fire. Down went the big bull, and I thought my task was done. But as I went back to mount the sorrel, he struggled to his feet again and disappeared after his companion among the trees, which were thicker here, as we had reached the bottom of the valley. So I tore after him again, and in a minute came to a dry watercourse. Scrambling into and out of this I saw the giraffes ahead of me just beginning the ascent of the opposite slope; and touching the horse with the spur we flew after the wounded bull. This time I made up my mind I would get up close enough; but Tranquillity did not quite like the look of the thing ahead of him. He did not refuse to come up to the giraffe, but he evidently felt that, with such an object close by and evident in the landscape, it behooved him to be careful as to what might be hidden therein, and he shied so at each bush we passed that we progressed in series of loops. So off I jumped, throwing the reins over his head, and opened fire once more; and this time the great bull went down for good.

Tranquillity recovered his nerve at once and grazed contentedly while I admired the huge proportions and beautiful coloring of my prize. In a few minutes Captain Slatter loped up, and the gun-bearers and saises followed. As if by magic, three or four Wakamba turned up immediately afterward, their eyes glistening at the thought of the feast ahead for the whole tribe. It was mid-afternoon, and there was no time to waste. My sais, Simba, an excellent long-distance runner, was sent straight to camp to get Heller and pilot him back to the dead giraffes. Beside each of the latter, for they had fallen a mile apart, we left a couple of men to build fires. Then we rode toward camp.

Next page: Edmund Heller, *Wakamba at Captain Slatter's*, Kilima Kiu, May 1909

Activities in and around Nairobi

Within the first three weeks of their safari the Roosevelts had already collected a wide variety of specimens, including several lions, giraffes, zebra, cheetah, hyenas, reedbucks, gazelles, and a rhinoceros. Sending his first article and a selection of Kermit's photographs to Robert Bridges, the assistant editor at *Scribner's Magazine*, on May 12, Roosevelt affixed a letter explaining, "I have had great luck; the game has come more quickly than I thought. Indeed, it has been almost too quick; I have had no time to write."

While hunting remained their focus, the Roosevelts took time away from the field periodically to engage in other activities, to rest, and to allow their frequently overtaxed party to attend to neglected duties, to resupply, and to rest themselves. On various occasions over the next eight months they spent their days in and around Nairobi. There many people sought out their company, and although social invitations irritated Roosevelt at times, he accepted many. Leaving the Kapiti and Athi Plains in mid-May, he and Kermit visited over the next three weeks the homes of prominent English and American settlers, including William McMillan, Hugh Heatley, and Ted and Helen Sanderson, all of whom lived in Nairobi or its outskirts.

Roosevelt also took an interest in the region's industrial and social development and often visited and wrote about new projects and organizations. While in Nairobi that spring he toured three different American and European missions in the area. These organizations' importance was growing during this period, and though many Africans complained about their presence, Roosevelt endorsed the religious, educational, and social work that the missionaries were doing.

09 May 12 to June 4, 1909

The English rule in Africa has been of incalculable benefit to Africans themselves, and indeed this is true of the rule of most European nations. Mistakes have been made, of course, but they have proceeded at least as often from an unwise effort to accomplish too much in the way of beneficence as from a desire to exploit the natives. Each of the civilized nations that has taken possession of any part of Africa has had its own peculiar good qualities and its own peculiar defects. Some of them have done too much in supervising and ordering the lives of the natives, and in interfering with their practices and customs. The English error, like our own under similar conditions, has, if anything, been in the other direction. The effort has been to avoid wherever possible all interference

Unidentified photographer, *American Steel Railroad Bridge at Kijabe. Roosevelt Was Much Interested in This*, June 1909

with tribal customs, even when of an immoral and repulsive character, and to do no more than what is obviously necessary, such as insistence upon keeping the peace and preventing the spread of cattle disease. Excellent reasons can be advanced in favor of this policy, and it must always be remembered that a fussy and ill-considered benevolence is more sure to awaken resentment than cruelty itself; while the natives are apt to resent deeply even things that are obviously for their ultimate welfare. Yet I cannot help thinking that with caution and wisdom it would be possible to proceed somewhat farther than has yet been the case in the direction of pushing upward some at least of the East African tribes: and this though I recognize fully that many of these tribes are of a low and brutalized type. Having said this much in the way of criticism, I wish to add my tribute of unstinted admiration for the disinterested and efficient work being done, alike in the interest of the white man and the black, by the government officials whom I met in East Africa. They are men in whom their country has every reason to feel a just pride.

We lunched with the American missionaries. Mission work among savages offers many difficulties, and often the wisest and most earnest effort meets with dishearteningly little reward; while lack of common sense, and of course, above all, lack of a firm and resolute disinterestedness, insures the worst kind of failure. There are missionaries who do not do well, just as there are men

Unidentified photographer, *Theodore Roosevelt, R. J. Cuninghame, and Edgar A. Mearns, en Route to Kijabe*, June 3, 1909

in every conceivable walk of life who do not do well; and excellent men who are not missionaries, including both government officials and settlers, are only too apt to jump at the chance of criticizing a missionary for every alleged sin of either omission or commission. Finally, zealous missionaries, fervent in the faith, do not always find it easy to remember that savages can only be raised by slow steps, that an empty adherence to forms and ceremonies amounts to nothing, that industrial training is an essential in any permanent upward movement, and that the gradual elevation of mind and character is a prerequisite to the achievement of any kind of Christianity which is worth calling such. Nevertheless, after all this has been said, it remains true that the good done by missionary effort in Africa has been incalculable.

Unidentified photographer, *Newland, Tarlton, & Company in Nairobi*, 1909

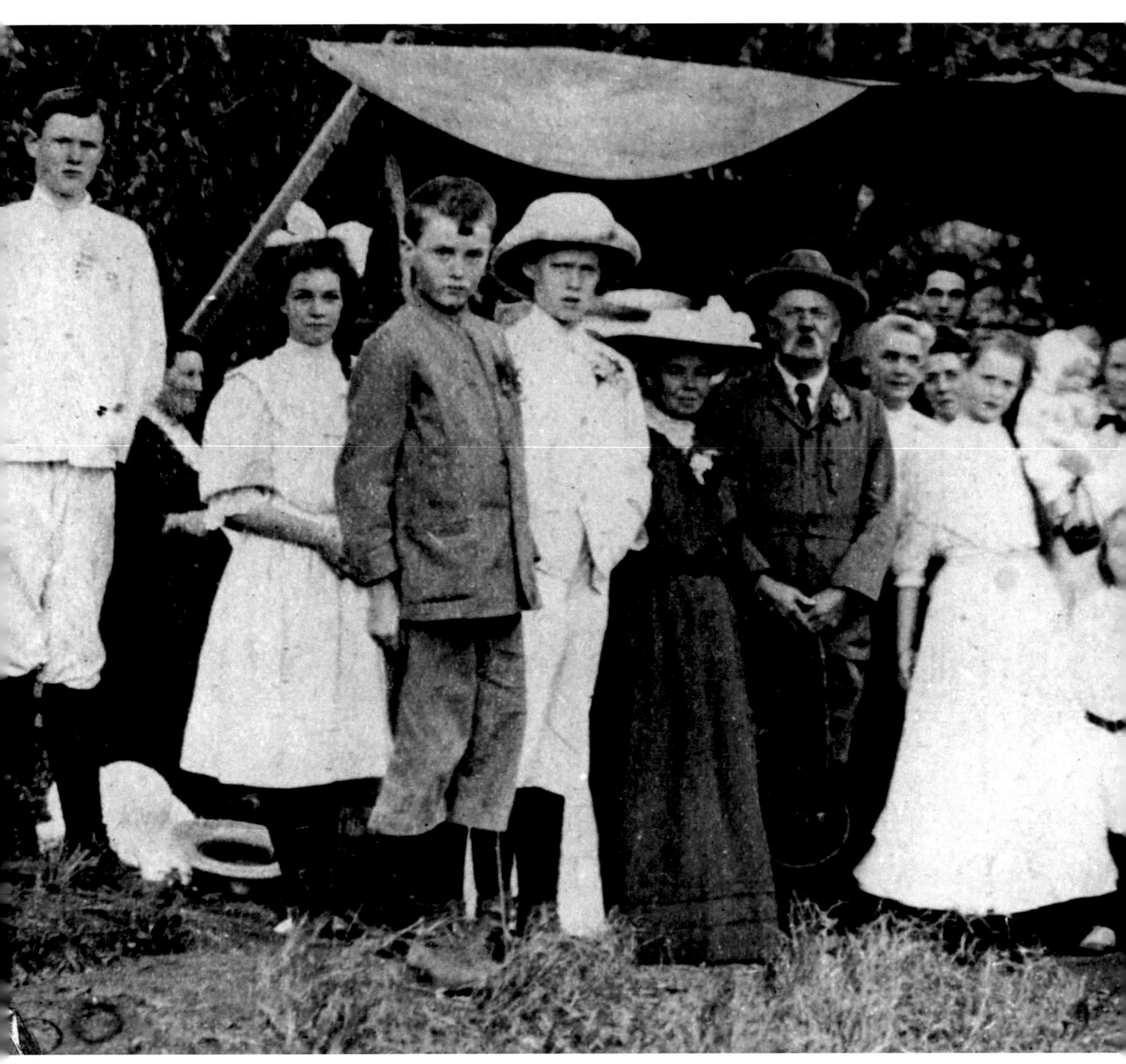

Kermit Roosevelt, *Mr. Roosevelt, the Missionaries, Their Wives and Children at the American Industrial Mission at Kijabe*, June 4, 1909

Birds at Hugh Heatley's Ranch

On his first trip to Africa as a boy, Roosevelt was fascinated by the continent's bird life. Having recently learned to shoot, he collected an assortment of specimens that he brought home. This passion for birds remained a constant throughout his life.

His expedition compatriot Edgar Mearns was also an experienced bird collector. A founding member of the American Ornithologists Union, he had traveled throughout the United States, as well as Mexico and the Philippines, in his work as a US Army surgeon. At each posting, he spent time studying and collecting birds. Praised by Smithsonian Secretary Charles Walcott as "the best field naturalist and collector in the United States," Mearns proved a great colleague in East Africa. With Roosevelt's support, he led the effort to collect birds, ultimately securing more than four thousand specimens. Collecting was a priority, but as important was the documentation of their habitats and customs. Each kept catalogues and descriptive notes about their observations.

While visiting British settler Hugh Heatley's ranch in Kamiti, ten miles northeast of Nairobi, in late May, Roosevelt had an opportunity to witness a variety of birds. Of special interest at this time was the black whydah finch, whose dancing captivated the former president.

 **Late May 1909**

Heatley's ranch comprises twenty thousand acres lying between the Rewero and Kamiti Rivers. It is seventeen miles long, and four across at the widest place. It includes some as beautiful bits of natural scenery as can well be imagined, and though Heatley—a thorough farmer, and the son and grandson of farmers—was making it a successful farm, with large herds of cattle, much improved stock, hundreds of acres under cultivation, a fine dairy, and the like, yet it was also a game reserve such as could not be matched either in Europe or America. . . .

There were interesting birds, too. Close by the woods at the river's edge, we saw a big black ground hornbill walking about, on the lookout for its usual dinner of small snakes and lizards. Large flocks of the beautiful Kavirondo cranes stalked over the plains and cultivated fields, or flew by with mournful, musical clangor. But the most interesting birds we saw were the black whydah finches. The female is a dull-colored, ordinary-looking bird, somewhat like a female bobolink. The male in

J. Alden Loring, *Vulture Raven or White-Necked Raven*, 1909

his courtship dress is clad in a uniform dark glossy suit, and his tail-feathers are almost like some of those of a barn-yard rooster, being over twice as long as the rest of the bird, with a downward curve at the tips. The females were generally found in flocks, in which there would often be a goodly number of males also, and when the flocks put on speed the males tended to drop behind. The flocks were feeding in Heatley's grain-fields, and he was threatening vengeance upon them. I was sorry, for the male birds certainly have habits of peculiar interest. They were not shy, although if we approached too near them in their favorite haunts, the grassland adjoining the papyrus beds, they would fly off and perch on the tops of the papyrus stems. The long tail hampers the bird in its flight, and it is often held at rather an angle downward, giving the bird a peculiar and almost insect-like appearance. But the marked and extraordinary peculiarity was the custom the cocks had of dancing in artificially made dancing-rings. For a mile and a half beyond our camp, down the course of the Kamiti, the grassland at the edge of the papyrus was thickly strewn with these dancing-rings. Each was about two feet in diameter, sometimes more, sometimes less. A tuft of growing grass perhaps a foot high was left in the center. Over the rest of the ring the grass was cut off close by the roots, and the blades strewn evenly over the surface of the ring. The cock bird would alight in the ring and hop to a height of a couple of feet, wings spread and motionless, tail drooping, and the head usually thrown back. As he came down, he might or might not give an extra couple of little hops. After a few seconds he would repeat the motion, sometimes remaining almost in the same place, at other times going forward during and between the hops so as finally to go completely round the ring. As there were many scores of these dancing-places within a comparatively limited territory, the effect was rather striking when a large number of birds were dancing at the same time. As one walked along, the impression conveyed by the birds continually popping above the grass and then immediately sinking back, was somewhat as if a man was making peas jump in a tin tray by tapping on it. The favorite dancing times were in the early morning, and, to a less extent, in the evening. We saw dancing-places of every age, some with the cut grass which strewed the floor green and fresh, others with the grass dried into hay and the bare earth showing through.

Unidentified photographer, *Wagtail*, 1909

Kermit Roosevelt, *Tohan and Marabou Stork*, 1909

Hunting Buffalo

Time away from the field also permitted Roosevelt to maintain correspondence with family, friends, and associates. An avid writer, he was especially active whenever he was near a place where mail could be sent. His wife, children and two sisters were regular recipients. Tales of his hunting success were largely absent in letters to his family; instead, updates about his health and comfort and about Kermit's well-being took center stage. Kermit's youthful exuberance was a source of both pride and concern at this time, as he related in a letter to his oldest son Ted on May 17: "It is hard to realize that the rather timid boy of four years ago has turned out a perfectly cool and daring fellow. Indeed, he is a little too reckless and keeps my heart in my throat, for I worry about him all the time; he is not a good shot, nor even as good as I am, and Heaven knows I am poor enough; but he is a bold rider, always cool and fearless, and eager to work all day long."

While in Nairobi, Roosevelt also wrote industrialist Andrew Carnegie, former Secretary of State Elihu Root, and Smithsonian Secretary Charles Walcott about the expedition's finances. During the first month of the safari, it had become apparent that he had underestimated its costs, and he wrote these three men asking for their assistance. In particular, he sought $30,000, as he wrote to Carnegie, "to enable the scientific expedition to continue until we reach Khartoum next March." While he assured him that he was underwriting his and Kermit's expenses, he explained that without these funds the Smithsonian naturalists "will have to go home and the scientific expedition [will] come to an end. . . . Now I feel that it would be a real misfortune to have this happen, from the standpoint of science in America." At the end of July, only a few days before his self-imposed deadline for securing these funds, he received word from Walcott that they would be able to continue without interruption. The expedition's financial supporters were not publicized at the time, though Walcott released their names in 1913 after questions about the project's funding had become public.

While at Heatley's, in addition to birding, Roosevelt also participated in his first African buffalo hunt. The addition of several Cape buffalo to his list of kills was a priority, though he recognized the danger associated with hunting this large and powerful mammal and worried about his and Kermit's safety. As Roosevelt wrote, "The list of white hunters that have been killed by buffalo is very long, and includes a number of men of note, while accidents to natives are of constant occurrence."

Kermit Roosevelt, *Hugh Heatley and a Buffalo Path*, May 1909

 **Late May 1909**

The game we were after was the buffalo herd that haunted the papyrus swamp. As I have said before, the buffalo is by many hunters esteemed the most dangerous of African game. It is an enormously powerful beast with, in this country, a coat of black hair which becomes thin in the old bulls, and massive horns which rise into great bosses at the base, these bosses sometimes meeting in old age so as to cover the forehead with a frontlet of horn. Their habits vary much in different places. Where they are much persecuted, they lie in the densest cover, and only venture out into the open to feed at night. But Heatley, though he himself had killed a couple of bulls, and the Boer farmer who was working for him another, had preserved the herd from outside molestation, and their habits were doubtless much what they would have been in regions where man is a rare visitor.

The first day we were on Heatley's farm, we saw the buffalo, to the number of seventy or eighty, grazing in the open, some hundreds of yards from the papyrus swamp, and this shortly after noon. For a mile from the papyrus swamp the country was an absolutely flat plain, gradually rising into a gentle slope, and it was an impossibility to approach the buffalo across this plain save in one way to be mentioned hereafter. Probably when the moon was full the buffalo came out to graze by night. But while we were on our hunt the moon was young, and the buffalo evidently spent most of the night in the papyrus and came out to graze by day. Sometimes they came out in the early morning, sometimes in the late evening, but quite as often in the bright daylight. We saw herds come out to graze at ten o'clock in the morning, and again at three in the afternoon. They usually remained out several hours, first grazing and then lying down. Flocks of the small white cow-heron usually accompanied them, the birds stalking about among them or perching on their backs; and occasionally the whereabouts of the herd in the papyrus swamp could be determined by seeing the flock of herons perched on the papyrus tops. We did not see any of the red-billed tickbirds on the buffalo; indeed, the only ones that we saw in this neighborhood happened to be on domestic cattle—in other places we found them very common on rhinoceros. At night the buffalo sometimes came right into the cultivated fields, and even into the garden close by the Boer farmer's house; and once at night he had shot a bull. The bullet went through the heart, but the animal ran to the papyrus swamp and was found next day dead just within the edge. Usually the main herd, of bulls, cows, and calves, kept together; but there were outlying bulls found singly or in small parties. Not only the natives but the whites were inclined to avoid the immediate neighborhood of the papyrus swamp, for there had been one or two narrow escapes from unprovoked attacks by the buffalo. . . .

The morning after making our camp, we started at dawn for the buffalo ground, Kermit and I, Cuninghame and Heatley, and the Boer farmer with three big, powerful dogs. We walked near the edge of the swamp. The whydah birds were continually bobbing up and down in front of us as they rose and fell on their dancing-places, while the Kavirondo cranes called mournfully all around. Before we had gone two miles, buffalo were spied, well ahead, feeding close to the papyrus. The line of the papyrus which marked the edge of the swamp was not straight but broken by projections and indentations; and by following it closely and cutting cautiously across the points, the opportunity for stalking was good. As there was not a tree of any kind anywhere near, we had to rely purely on our shooting to prevent damage from the buffalo. Kermit and I had our double-barrels, with the Winchesters as spare guns, while Cuninghame carried a 577, and Heatley a magazine rifle.

Unidentified photographer, *Mr. Roosevelt and Kermit Roosevelt with the First Buffalo*, May 1909

Unidentified photographer, *Cuninghame, Self, Father, Heller, and Heatley at Buffalo Camp*, May 1909

Cautiously threading our way along the edge of the swamp, we got within a hundred and fifty yards of the buffalo before we were perceived. There were four bulls, grazing close by the edge of the swamp, their black bodies glistening in the early sunrays, their massive horns showing white, and the cow-herons perched on their backs. They stared sullenly at us with outstretched heads from under their great frontlets of horn. The biggest of the four stood a little out from the other three, and at him I fired, the bullet telling with a smack on the tough hide and going through the lungs. We had been afraid they would at once turn into the papyrus, but instead of this they started straight across our front directly for the open country.

This was a piece of huge good luck. Kermit put his first barrel into the second bull, and I my second barrel into one of the others, after which it became impossible to say which bullet struck which animal, as the firing became general. They ran a quarter of a mile into the open, and then the big bull I had first shot, and which had no other bullet in him, dropped dead, while the other three, all of which were wounded, halted beside him. We walked toward them, rather expecting a charge; but when we were still over two hundred yards away, they started back for the swamp, and we began firing. The distance being long, I used my Winchester. Aiming well before one bull, he dropped to the shot as if pole-axed, falling straight on his back with his legs kicking; but in a moment he was up again and after the others. Later I found that the bullet, a full-metal patch, had struck him in the head but did not penetrate to the brain, and merely stunned him for the moment. All the time we kept running diagonally to their line of flight. They were all three badly wounded, and when they reached the tall rank grass, high as a man's head, which fringed the papyrus swamp, the two foremost lay down, while the last one, the one I had floored with the Winchester, turned, and with nose outstretched began to come toward us. He was badly crippled, however, and with a soft-nosed bullet from my heavy Holland I knocked him down, this time for good. The other two then rose, and though each was again hit they reached the swamp, one of them to our right, the other to the left where the papyrus came out in a point.

We decided to go after the latter, and advancing very cautiously toward the edge of the swamp, put in the three big dogs. A moment after, they gave tongue within the papyrus; then we heard the savage grunt of the buffalo and saw its form just within the reeds; and as the rifles cracked, down it went. But it was not dead, for we heard it grunt savagely, and the dogs bayed as loudly as ever. Heatley now mounted his trained shooting-pony and rode toward the place, while we covered him with our rifles, his plan being to run right across our front if the bull charged. The bull was past charging, lying just within the reeds, but he was still able to do damage, for in another minute one of the dogs came out by us and ran straight back to the farmhouse, where we found him dead on our return. He had been caught by the buffalo's horns when he went in too close. Heatley, a daring fellow, with great confidence in both his horse and his rifle, pushed forward as we came up, and saw the bull lying on the ground while the two other dogs bit and worried it; and he put a bullet through its head.

The remaining bull got off into the swamp, where a week later Heatley found his dead body. Fortunately, the head proved to be in less good condition than any of the others, as one horn was broken off about half-way up; so that if any of the four had to escape, it was well that this should have been the one.

Edmund Heller, *Porters Dancing When Breaking Camp at Kamiti*, May 1909

Our three bulls were fine trophies. The largest, with the largest horns, was the first killed, being the one that fell to my first bullet; yet it was the youngest of the three. The other two were old bulls. The second one killed had smaller horns than the other, but the bosses met in the middle of the forehead for a space of several inches, making a solid shield. I had just been reading a pamphlet by a German specialist who had divided the African buffalo into fifteen or twenty different species, based upon differences in various pairs of horns. The worth of such fine distinctions, when made on insufficient data, can be gathered from the fact that on the principles of specific division adopted in the pamphlet in question, the three bulls we had shot would have represented certainly two and possibly three different species.

Through the Thirst to the Sotik

The Roosevelts left their hosts in and around Nairobi and set out on the next segment of their safari in early June. Over the next five weeks they spent their time west and south of Nairobi in various places, including the Sotik, an arid region that was home to the Maasai. There they continued to find plentiful game to hunt.

Back in the United States and elsewhere, news about the safari circulated widely. In Nairobi, Roosevelt had recently reencountered Francis W. Dawson of the United Press and W. Robert Foran of the Associated Press and reluctantly permitted them to join the expedition for short intervals. Dawson later recalled their exchange: "I told him my frank opinion that he had no choice but to let the public have occasional authentic news. It could be as much or as little as he thought proper." Though eyewitness reports were better than fictitious rumors, the stories acted to heighten interest in his travels and at times precipitated new controversies.

Roosevelt's longtime adversary William J. Long resurfaced at this time and criticized the former president's hunting again in *the New York Times*:

> He is a game butcher pure and simple, and his interest in animals lies chiefly in the direction of blood and brutality. . . . The worst feature in the whole bloody business is not the killing of a few hundred wild animals in Africa, but the brutalizing influence which these reports have upon thousands of American boys. Only last week I met half a dozen little fellows in the woods. The biggest boy had a gun and a squirrel's tail in his hat and he called himself Bwana Tumbo. They were shooting everything in sight, killing birds at a time when every dead mother meant a nestful of young birds slowly starving to death. How could I convince them that their work is inhumane? Is not the great American hero occupied at this time with the same detestable business?

At times Roosevelt heard reports about goings-on back at home, though he tried to steer clear of any news except for items mentioned in letters from family and friends. As Dawson observed, "he wanted rest from his usual preoccupations, and freedom to hunt in the wilds—nothing more."

12　June 5 to July 9, 1909

On June 5th we started south from Kijabe to trek through the thirst, through the waterless country which lies across the way to the Sotik. . . .

The trek across "the thirst," as any waterless country is apt to be called by an Africander, is about sixty miles, by the road. On our horses we could have ridden it in a night; but on a serious trip of any kind loads must be carried, and laden porters cannot go fast, and must rest at intervals. We had rather more than our porters could carry, and needed additional transportation for the water for the safari; and we had hired four ox wagons. . . .

We had one hundred and ninety-six porters, in addition to the askaris, tent boys, gun-bearers, and saises. The management of such a safari is a work of difficulty; but no better man for the purpose than Cuninghame could be found anywhere, and he had chosen his headmen well. In the thirst, the march goes on by day and night. The longest halt is made in the day, for men and animals both travel better at night than under the blazing noon. We were fortunate in that it was just after the full of the moon, so that our night treks were made in good light. Of course, on such a march the porters must be spared as much as possible; camp is not pitched, and each white man uses for the trip only what he wears or carries on his horse—and the horse also must be loaded as lightly as possible. I took nothing but my army overcoat, rifle and cartridges, and three canteens of water. Kermit did the same.

The wagons broke camp about ten, to trek to the water, a mile and a half off, where the oxen would be outspanned to take the last drink for three days; stock will not drink early in the morning nearly as freely as if the march is begun later. We, riding our horses, followed by the long line of burdened porters, left at half-past twelve, and in a couple of hours overtook the wagons. The porters were in high spirits. In the morning, before the start, they twice held regular dances, the chief musician being one of their own number who carried an extraordinary kind of native harp; and after their loads were allotted they marched out of camp singing and blowing their horns and whistles. Three askaris brought up the rear to look after laggards and see that no weak or sick man fell out without our knowing or being able to give him help.

The trail led first through open brush, or low, dry forest, and then out on the vast plains, where the withered grass was dotted here and there with low, scantily leaved thorn-trees, from three to eight feet high. Hour after hour we drew slowly ahead under the shimmering sunlight. The horsemen walked first, with the gun-bearers, saises, and usually a few very energetic and powerful porters; then came the safari in single file; and then the lumbering white-topped wagons, the patient oxen walking easily, each team led by a half-naked savage with frizzed hair

Unidentified photographer, *Theodore Roosevelt Starting Out on His Horse* Tranquillity *to Cross the Great Thirst Belt for Hunting Grounds in the Sotik*, June 5, 1909

and a spear or throwing-stick in his hand, while at intervals the long whips of the drivers cracked like rifles. The dust rose in clouds from the dry earth, and soon covered all of us; in the distance herds of zebra and hartebeest gazed at us as we passed, and we saw the old spoor of rhino, beasts we hoped to avoid, as they often charge such a caravan.

Slowly the shadows lengthened; the light waned, the glare of the white, dusty plain was softened, and the bold outlines of the distant mountains grew dim. Just before nightfall we halted on the further side of a dry watercourse. The safari came up singing and whistling, and the men put down their loads, lit fires, and with chatter and laughter prepared their food. The crossing was not good, the sides of the watercourse being steep; and each wagon was brought through by a double span, the whips cracking lustily as an accompaniment to the shouts of the drivers, as the thirty oxen threw their weight into the yokes by which they were attached to the long trek tow. The horses were fed. We had tea, with bread and cold meat—and a most delicious meal it was—and then lay dozing or talking beside the bushfires. At half-past eight, the moon

113

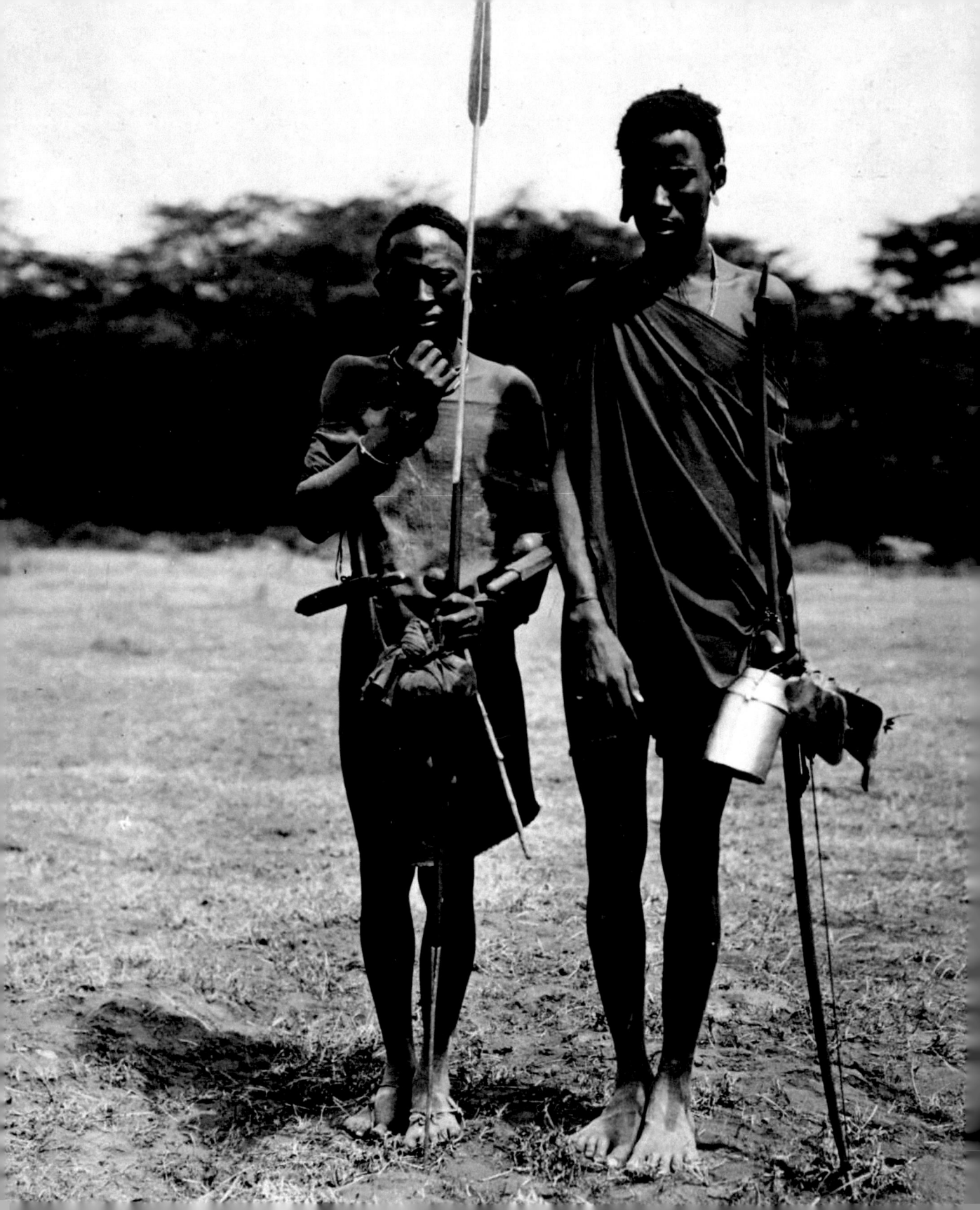

having risen, we were off again. The safari was still in high spirits and started with the usual chanting and drumming.

We pushed steadily onward across the plain, the dust rising in clouds under the spectral moonlight. Sometimes we rode, sometimes we walked to ease our horses. The Southern Cross was directly ahead, not far above the horizon. Higher and higher rose the moon, and brighter grew the flood of her light. At intervals the barking call of zebras was heard on either hand. It was after midnight when we again halted. The porters were tired and did not sing as they came up; the air was cool, almost nipping, and they at once huddled down in their blankets, some of them building fires. We, the white men, after seeing our horses staked out, each lay down in his overcoat or jacket and slicker, with his head on his saddle, and his rifle beside him, and had a little over two hours' sleep. At three we were off again, the shivering porters making no sound as they started; but once under way the more irrepressible spirits speedily began a kind of intermittent chant, and most of the rest by degrees joined in the occasional grunt or hum that served as chorus.

For four hours we travelled steadily, first through the moonlight, and then through the reddening dawn. Jackals shrieked, and the plains plover wailed and scolded as they circled round us. When the sun was well up, we halted; the desolate flats stretched far and wide on every side and rose into lofty hills ahead of us. The porters received their water and food, and lay down to sleep, some directly in the open, others rigging little sun shelters under the scattering thornbushes. The horses were fed, were given half a pail of water apiece, and were turned loose to graze with the oxen; this was the last time the oxen would feed freely, unless there was rain; and this was to be our longest halt. We had an excellent breakfast, like our supper the night before, and then slept as well as we could.

Noon came, and soon afterward we again started. The country grew hilly, and brushy. It was too dry for much game, but we saw a small herd of giraffe, which are independent of water. Now riding our horses, now leading them, we travelled until nearly sunset, when we halted at the foot of a steep divide, beyond which our course lay across slopes that gradually fell to the stream for which we were heading. Here the porters had all the food and water they wished, and so did the horses; and, each with a double span of oxen, the wagons were driven up the slope, the weary cattle straining hard in the yokes.

Black clouds had risen and thickened in the west, boding rain. Three-fourths of our journey was over; and it was safe to start the safari and then leave it to come on by itself, while the ox

Edmund Heller, *Maasai Guides on the Sotik Trip*, June 1909

Next page: Unidentified photographer, *Photographing a Lion in the Sotik*, June 1909

wagons followed later. At nine, before the moon struggled above the hillcrests to our left, we were off. Soon we passed the wagons, drawn up abreast, a lantern high on a pole, while the tired oxen lay in their yokes, attached to the trek tow. An hour afterward we left the safari behind, and rode ahead, with only our saises and gunbearers. Gusts of rain blew in our faces, and gradually settled into a steady, gentle downpour. Our horses began to slip in the greasy soil; we knew the rain would refresh the cattle but would make the going harder.

At one we halted, in the rain, for a couple of hours' rest. Just before this we heard two lions roaring, or rather grunting, not far in front of us; they were after prey. Lions are bold on rainy nights, and we did not wish to lose any of our horses; so a watch was organized, and we kept ready for immediate action, but the lions did not come. The native boys built fires, and lay close to them, relieving one another, and us, as sentinels. Kermit and I had our army overcoats, which are warm and practically waterproof; the others had coats almost as good. We lay down in the rain, on the drenched grass, with our saddlecloths over our feet, and our heads on our saddles, and slept comfortably for two hours.

At three we mounted and were off again, the rain still falling. There were steep ravines to cross, slippery from the wet; but we made good time, and soon after six off-saddled on the farther side of a steep drift or ford in the little Suavi River. It is a rapid stream flowing between high, well-wooded banks; it was an attractive camp site, and, as we afterward found, the nights were so cool as to make great campfires welcome. At half-past ten the safari appeared, in excellent spirits, the flag waving, to an accompaniment of chanting and horn-blowing; and, to their loudly expressed satisfaction, the porters were told that they should have an extra day's rations, as well as a day's rest. Camp was soon pitched; and all, of every rank, slept soundly that night, though the lions moaned nearby.

Unidentified photographer, *Theodore Roosevelt Reading in Front of His Tent in Camp at Kijabe*, June 1909

Next page: Edmund Heller, *A Great Candelabrum Euphorbia by Our Camp*, June 1909

Visit to a Maasai Kraal

The Maasai have historically inhabited lands within and around the Sotik. Pastoralists, they have long depended upon cattle as their primary food source. In Roosevelt's day, the Maasai faced pressure on their homelands from neighboring rival groups, as well as British colonial authorities who sought to create wildlife reserves and parks in the region.

During their time on the Sotik, the expedition encountered several Maasai villages, called *kraal*. A brush and mud wall surrounded these communities to protect the inhabitants and their livestock from predatory animals. The Maasai they met were generally friendly toward the Roosevelt party, and on one occasion organized a traditional spear dance for their entertainment. Unable to communicate without an interpreter, the former president showed only passing interest in the Maasai and their villages. He described the clothing and adornment of their men and women, but explained little about their customs, manners, and present-day challenges. As one well versed in ancient Egyptian history, Roosevelt saw the Maasai not for what they were then, but rather in comparison to an African civilization that had existed more than three thousand years earlier.

 ## Late June 1909

Four miles from camp was a Maasai kraal, and we went toward this when we caught the gleam of the fires; for the porters were getting exhausted. The kraal was in shape a big oval, with a thick wall of thornbushes, eight feet high, the low huts standing just within this wall, while the cattle and sheep were crowded into small bomas in the center. The fires gleamed here and there within, and as we approached, we heard the talking and laughing of men and women, and the lowing and bleating of the pent-up herds and flocks. We hailed loudly, explaining our needs. At first, they were very suspicious. They told us we could not bring the lion within, because it would frighten the cattle, but after some parley consented to our building a fire outside and skinning the animal. They passed two brands over the thorn fence, and our men speedily kindled a blaze, and drew the lioness beside it. By this time the Maasai were reassured, and a score of their warriors, followed soon by half a dozen women, came out through a small opening in the fence, and crowded close around

Unidentified photographer, *Maasai Warriors*, June or July 1909

Next page: Unidentified photographer, *Maasai Kraal, Mau Escarpment*, July 10, 1909

Edmund Heller, *Maasai Huts from Center of Kraal,* June or July 1909

the fire, with boisterous, noisy good humor. They showed a tendency to chaff our porters. One, the humorist of the crowd, excited much merriment by describing, with pantomimic accompaniment of gestures, how when the white man shot a lion it might bite a swahili, who thereupon would call for his mother. But they were entirely friendly and offered me calabashes of milk. The men were tall, finely shaped savages, their hair plastered with red mud, and drawn out into longish ringlets; they were naked except for a blanket worn, not round the loins, but over the shoulders; their ears were slit, and from them hung bone and wooden ornaments; they wore metal bracelets and anklets, and chains which passed around their necks, or else over one side of the neck and under the opposite arm. The women had pleasant faces and were laden with metal ornaments—chiefly wire anklets, bracelets, and necklaces—of many pounds weight. The features of the men were bold and clear-cut, and their bearing warlike and self-reliant; as the flame of the fire glanced over them, and brought their faces and bronze figures into lurid relief against the darkness, the likeness was striking, not to the West Coast negroes, but to the engravings on the tombs, temples, and palaces of ancient Egypt; they might have been soldiers in the armies of Thothmes or Rameses. They stood resting on their long staffs, and looked at me as I leaned on my rifle; and they laughed and jested with their women, who felt the lion's teeth and claws and laughed back at the men; our gun-bearers worked at the skinning, and answered the jests of their warlike friends with the freedom of men who themselves followed a dangerous trade; the two horses stood quiet just outside the circle; and over all the firelight played and leaped.

Unidentified photographer, *Maasai Woman and Toto,* June or July 1909

With the Attenboroughs at Lake Naivasha

After five weeks on the Sotik, the safari marched north toward Lake Naivasha beginning on July 10. Located about sixty miles northwest of Nairobi, it is a large lake that abounds in bird life and is famous for its population of hippopotamuses. Retired British naval officer Frederick Attenborough and his brother Henry owned a farm on the shores of Lake Naivasha and were pleased to welcome the former president and his party. For the next two weeks, the safari hunted in this area. Though Roosevelt was sidelined for several days with a fever—his first and only illness of the trip—he and Kermit were successful in adding several hippopotamuses to their specimen collection.

Yet, the multiday hunt was not without controversy. Toward the end of their stay, Roosevelt went out on the lake looking to add a male to his collection and in a moment of confusion and panic killed four hippopotamuses. The episode left him distraught, and he worried about fresh accusations against him and his larger expedition. While he downplayed the issue in *African Game Trails*, journalist Francis W. Dawson, who was in camp at the time, recalled Roosevelt explaining to him: "A most awful thing has happened . . . I don't know what to do about it. We shall have to let the papers know. And this is *not* a game-slaughtering expedition." The episode was noticed in the newspapers, but it did not cause the uproar that Roosevelt had expected.

 ## July 10 to July 23, 1909

There were a number of hippo in these lagoons. One afternoon after four o'clock I saw two standing half out of water in a shallow, eating the water-lilies. They seemed to spend the fore part of the day sleeping or resting in the papyrus or near its edge; toward evening they splashed and waded among the waterlilies, tearing them up with their huge jaws; and during the night they came ashore to feed on the grass and land plants. In consequence those killed during the day, until the late afternoon, had their stomachs filled, not with water plants, but with grasses which they must have obtained in their night journeys on dry land. At night I heard the bulls bellowing and roaring. They fight savagely among themselves, and where they are not molested, and the natives are timid, they not only do great damage to the gardens and crops, trampling them down and shoveling basketfuls into their huge mouths, but also become dangerous to human beings, attacking boats or canoes in a spirit of wanton and ferocious mischief. At this place, a few weeks

Kermit Roosevelt, *Mr. Roosevelt's Hippo Charging Open-Mouthed*, July 1909

before our arrival, a young bull, badly scarred, and evidently having been mishandled by some bigger bull, came ashore in the daytime and actually attacked the cattle, and was promptly shot in consequence. They are astonishingly quick in their movements for such shapeless-looking, short-legged things. Of course they cannot swim in deep water with anything like the speed of the real swimming mammals, nor move on shore with the agility and speed of the true denizens of the land; nevertheless, by sheer muscular power and in spite of their shape, they move at an unexpected rate of speed both on dry land and in deep water; and in shallow water, their true home, they gallop very fast on the bottom, under water. Ordinarily only their heads can be seen, and they must be shot in the brain. If they are found in a pool with little cover, and if the shots can be taken close by, from firm ground, there is no sport whatever in killing them. But the brain is small and the skull huge, and if they are any distance off, and especially if the shot has to be taken from an unsteady boat, there is ample opportunity to miss.

On the day we spent with the big rowboat in the lagoons both Kermit and I had shots; each of us hit, but neither of us got his game. My shot was at the head of a hippo facing me in a bay about a hundred yards off, so that I had to try to shoot very low between the eyes; the water was smooth, and I braced my legs well and fired off-hand. I hit him, but was confident that I had missed the brain, for he lifted slightly, and then went under, nose last; and when a hippo is shot in the brain the head usually goes under nose first. An exasperating feature of hippo shooting is

J. Alden Loring, *Towing in Bull Hippo, Lake Naivasha*, July 1909

that, save in exceptional circumstances, where the water is very shallow, the animal sinks at once when killed outright, and does not float for one or two or three hours; so that one has to wait that length of time before finding out whether the game has or has not been bagged. On this occasion we never saw a sign of the animal after I fired, and as it seemed impossible that in that situation the hippo could get off unobserved, my companions thought I had killed him; I thought not, and unfortunately my judgment proved to be correct.

Another day, in the launch, I did much the same thing. Again, the hippo was a long distance off, only his head appearing, but unfortunately not in profile, much the best position for a shot; again I hit him; again he sank and, look as hard as we could, not a sign of him appeared, so that everyone was sure he was dead; and again nobody ever floated. But on this day Kermit got his hippo. He hit it first in the head, merely a flesh wound; but the startled creature then rose high in the water, and he shot it in the lungs. It now found difficulty in staying under, and continually rose to the surface with a plunge like a porpoise, going as fast as it could toward the papyrus. After it we went, full speed, for once in the papyrus we could not have followed it; and Kermit finally killed it, just before it reached the edge of the swamp, and, luckily, where the water was

Edmund Heller, *Bringing the Skin of the Large Hippo to Camp*, July 1909

so shallow that we did not have to wait for it to float, but fastened a rope to two of its turtle-like legs, and towed it back forthwith.

There were otters in the lake. One day we saw two playing together near the shore; and at first we were all of us certain that it was some big water snake. It was not until we were very close that we made out the supposed one big snake to be two otters; it was rather interesting, as giving one of the explanations of the stories that always appear about large water snakes, or similar monsters, existing in almost every lake of any size in a wild country. On another day I shot another near shore; he turned over and over, splashing and tumbling; but just as were to grasp him, he partially recovered and dived to safety in the reeds.

On the second day we went out in the launch I got my hippo. We steamed down the lake, not far from the shore, for over ten miles, dragging the big, clumsy rowboat, in which Cuninghame had put three of our porters who knew how to row. Then we spied a big hippo walking entirely out of water on the edge of the papyrus, at the farther end of a little bay which was filled with

Next page: Unidentified photographer, *Hippopotamus on Shore at Lake Naivasha*, July 1909

waterlilies. Thither we steamed, and when a few rods from the bay, Cuninghame, Kermit, and I got into the rowboat; Cuninghame steered, Kermit carried his camera, and I steadied myself in the bow with the little Springfield rifle. The hippo was a self-confident, truculent beast; it went under water once or twice, but again came out to the papyrus and waded along the edge, its body out of water. We headed toward it and thrust the boat in among the waterlilies, finding that the bay was shallow, from three to six feet deep. While still over a hundred yards from the hippo, I saw it turn as if to break into the papyrus, and at once fired into its shoulder, the tiny, pointed bullet smashing the big bones. Round spun the great beast, plunged into the water, and with its huge jaws open came straight for the boat, floundering and splashing through the thick-growing waterlilies. I think that its chief object was to get to deep water; but we were between it and the deep water, and instead of trying to pass to one side it charged straight for the boat, with open jaws, bent on mischief. But I hit it again and again with the little sharp-pointed bullet. Once I struck it between neck and shoulder; once, as it rushed forward with its huge jaws stretched to their threatening utmost, I fired right between them, whereat it closed them with the clash of a sprung bear trap; and then, when under the punishment it swerved for a moment, I hit it at the base of the ear, a brain shot which dropped it in its tracks. Meanwhile Kermit was busily taking photos of it as it charged, and, as he mentioned afterward, until it was dead he never saw it except in the "finder" of his camera. The water was so shallow where I had killed the hippo that its body projected slightly above the surface. It was the hardest kind of work getting it out from among the waterlilies; then we towed it to camp behind the launch.

The engineer of the launch was an Indian Moslem. The fireman and the steersman were two half-naked and much-ornamented Kikuyus. The fireman wore a blue bead chain on one ankle, a brass armlet on the opposite arm, a belt of short steel chains, a dingy blanket (no loin cloth), and a skullcap surmounted by a plume of ostrich feathers. The two Kikuyus were unconsciously entertaining companions. Without any warning they would suddenly start a song or chant, usually an impromptu recitative of whatever at the moment interested them. They chanted for half an hour over the feat of the "Bwana Makuba" (great master or chief, my name) in killing the hippo; laying especial stress upon the quantity of excellent meat it would furnish, and how very good the eating would be. Usually one would improvise the chant, and the other join in the chorus. Sometimes they would solemnly sing complimentary songs to one another, each in turn chanting the manifold good qualities of his companion.

Return to Nairobi

On July 24 the Roosevelts returned to Nairobi for a ten-day break. No hunting was conducted during this time. The naturalists used this period to prepare a second group of specimens for shipment back to Washington. The Roosevelts stayed with William N. McMillan, a wealthy St. Louis native and big-game hunter who owned a twenty-thousand-acre ranch in nearby Thika. McMillan also served as the chair of an entertainment committee meant to organize social events during the former president's visit. Though not hunting, Roosevelt was hardly inactive. He used his time to follow up on correspondence, write new installments for *Scribner's*, attend various dinners and a dance at the Nairobi Club, and deliver a speech on August 3, much anticipated by locals and the foreign press alike, about the British colonial enterprise in East Africa.

In his speech he expressed much optimism for the future, unlike Winston Churchill, who two years earlier had questioned British's involvement in Africa. Roosevelt encouraged British and American settlers to continue their work in developing the region, though he recommended that more lands be set aside as reserves for the protection of wildlife. He spoke about the African population and their future and conveyed the same patriarchal and racist attitudes common among the Anglo-American elite of the day: the "black man [should] be treated with justice and helped upward, not pressed downward. Brutality and injustice are especially hateful when exercised on the helpless. . . . The tribes hereabouts are of course hopelessly incompetent to better themselves or to utilize this country to advantage without white leadership and direction, and progress among them will be the work not of years but of many generations." In Roosevelt's eyes Africans remained inferior, no matter the extraordinary assistance and guidance they had provided over the past three months. In addition, although he commonly described the Indigenous communities he encountered, he shared little interest in trying to understand their unique cultures.

Horse racing was also a popular pursuit in Nairobi, and their visit coincided with the annual weeklong series of races. Large crowds gathered to witness, and Kermit agreed to participate in several races. In a letter to his daughter, Ethel, Roosevelt described how Kermit fared: "He has ridden with great good humor and courage in half a dozen races, always on poor horses, generally near the tail of the procession, but riding well and pluckily and in the best kind of sporting spirit."

Unidentified photographer, *Roosevelt in Nairobi*, August 3, 1909

15 **July 24 to August 3, 1909**

Most of the time in Nairobi we were the guests of ever-hospitable McMillan, in his low, cool house, with its broad, vine-shaded veranda, running around all four sides, and its garden, fragrant and brilliant with innumerable flowers. Birds abounded, singing beautifully; the bulbuls were the most noticeable singers, but there were many others. The dark ant-eating chats haunted the dusky roads on the outskirts of the town, and were interesting birds; they were usually found in parties, flirted their tails up and down as they sat on bushes or roofs or wires, sang freely in chorus until after dusk, and then retired to holes in the ground for the night. A tiny owl with a queer little voice called continually not only after nightfall, but in the bright afternoons. Shrikes spitted insects on the spines of the imported cactus in the gardens.

Left: Paul Thompson, *Roosevelt on His Favorite Horse* Tranquillity *in Nairobi*, July 26, 1909

Next page: Unidentified photographer, *William N. McMillan's Home*, 1909

It was race week, and the races, in some of which Kermit rode, were capital fun. The white people—army officers, government officials, farmers from the country roundabout, and their wives—rode to the races on ponies or even on camels, or drove up in rickshaws, in gharries, in bullock tongas, occasionally in automobiles, most often in two-wheel carts or rickety hacks drawn by mules and driven by a turbaned Indian or a native in a cotton shirt. There were Parsees, and Goanese dressed just like the Europeans. There were many other Indians, their picturesque women-kind gaudy in crimson, blue, and saffron. The constabulary, Indian and native, were in neat uniforms and well set up, though often barefooted. Straight, slender Somalis with clear-cut features were in attendance on the horses. Native negroes, of many different tribes, flocked to the racecourse and its neighborhood. The Swahilis, and those among the others who aspired toward civilization, were well clad, the men in half European costume, the women in flowing, parti-colored robes. But most of them were clad, or unclad, just as they always had been. Wakamba, with filed teeth, crouched in circles on the ground. Kikuyu passed, the men each with a blanket hung round the shoulders, and girdles of chains, and armlets and anklets of solid metal; the older women bent under burdens they carried on the back, half of them in addition with babies slung somewhere round them, while now and then an unmarried girl would have her face painted with ochre and vermilion. A small party of Maasai warriors kept close together, each clutching his shining, long-bladed war spear, their hair daubed red and twisted into strings. A large band of Kavirondo, stark naked, with shield and spear and head-dress of nodding plumes, held a dance near the racetrack. As for the races themselves, they were carried on in the most sporting spirit, and only the Australian poet Patterson could adequately write of them.

Explorations around Mount Kenya

On the day following his speech, Roosevelt departed Nairobi to begin an extended reconnaissance of the region around Mount Kenya, at 17,058 feet the second-highest mountain in Africa after Kilimanjaro. He traveled north with Dawson by rail to Kijabe, where he alighted for an hour to lay the cornerstone of a new building at the American Interdenominational Mission, before moving on toward the station at Lake Naivasha. Several days later the entire expedition reunited there and prepared for the next stage of their trip. On previous occasions members of the group had split apart from the main group for short periods to pursue specific collecting aims. In exploring the expansive terrain around and on Mount Kenya, they decided to divide into three parties and to work apart for several weeks. Roosevelt wished to focus attention on elephants, an animal he had not yet hunted, and Heller and Cuninghame joined him in this pursuit. Kermit and outfitter Leslie Tarlton led the second group, and Mearns and Loring the third.

While in search of elephants, Roosevelt's group remained attuned to smaller mammals and other botanical and ornithological specimens. In traversing new types of terrain—wetter, mountainous, and more forested—they encountered a wide assortment of plants and animals that caught their attention. Loring, as an expert in small mammals, took a special interest in mice, shrews, and other such creatures, though he was not alone.

 ## August 4 to September 20, 1909

Four days' march from Naivasha, where we again left Mearns and Loring, took us to Nyeri. Our line of march lay across the high plateaus and mountain chains of the Aberdare range. The steep, twisting trail was slippery with mud. Our last camp, at an altitude of about ten thousand feet, was so cold that the water froze in the basins, and the shivering porters slept in numbed discomfort. There was constant fog and rain, and on the highest plateau the bleak landscape, shrouded in driving mist, was northern to all the senses. The ground was rolling, and through the deep valleys ran brawling brooks of clear water; one little foaming stream, suddenly tearing down a hill-side, might have been that which Childe Roland crossed before he came to the dark tower.

Unidentified photographer, *Father Lays Corner Stone at Kijabe Mission*, August 4, 1909

There was not much game, and it generally moved abroad by night. One frosty evening we killed a duiker by shining its eyes. We saw old elephant tracks. The high, wet levels swarmed with mice and shrews, just as our arctic and alpine meadows swarm with them. The species were really widely different from ours, but many of them showed curious analogies in form and habits; there was a short-tailed shrew much like our mole shrew, and a long-haired, short-tailed rat like a very big meadow mouse. They were so plentiful that we frequently saw them, and the grass was cut up by their runways. They were abroad during the day, probably finding the nights too cold, and in an hour, Heller trapped a dozen or two individuals belonging to seven species and five different genera. There were not many birds so high up. There were deer ferns; and Spanish moss hung from the trees and even from the bamboos. The flowers

Unidentified photographer, *Elephant Shrew*, 1909

included utterly strange forms, as for instance giant lobelias ten feet high. Others we know in our gardens; geraniums and red-hot pokers, which in places turned the glades to a fire color. Yet others either were like, or looked like, our own wildflowers: orange lady-slippers, red gladiolus on stalks six feet high, pansy-like violets, and blackberries and yellow raspberries. There were stretches of bushes bearing masses of small red or large white flowers shaped somewhat like columbines, or like the garden balsam; the red flower bushes were under the bamboos, the white at a lower level. The crests and upper slopes of the mountains were clothed in the green uniformity of the bamboo forest, the trail winding dim under its dark archway of tall, close-growing stems. Lower down were junipers and yews, and then many other trees, with among them tree ferns and strange dragon-trees with lily-like frondage. Zone succeeded zone from top to bottom, each marked by a different plant life.

Unidentified photographer, *J. Alden Loring with Elephant Shrew*, 1909

Kikuyu Dance at Nyeri

As they trekked northeast from Lake Naivasha across the Aberdare Range toward Mount Kenya, Roosevelt's party stopped in the village of Nyeri. There on two different occasions under the direction of Governor Jackson the local Kikuyu tribespeople organized a series of dances for the former president. Dressed in traditional regalia and holding richly painted shields and spears, approximately two thousand participants performed. Kermit was on hand to photograph the first dance. At the second performance twelve days later, James L. Clark, a naturalist from the American Museum of Natural History, and his traveling companion, British filmmaker Cherry Kearton, joined Roosevelt to witness the event. Though Roosevelt had been uninterested in the type of publicity film that William Selig had wanted to create, he welcomed Clark and Kearton at his camp and agreed to pose before the film camera. Whereas Kearton had secured only a small amount of footage when they first met in Mombasa, he completed 450 feet of film at Nyeri, highlights of which appeared in *Roosevelt in Africa*, the movie about East Africa that Kearton released the following April. Unlike Selig's fictitious drama *Hunting Big Game in Africa*, Kearton's movie—although it featured authentic footage—failed to attract a wide audience, and within weeks it was pulled from theaters. Kearton was a supporter of Roosevelt's, and later, in recognition of his contributions to conservation, he dedicated one of his books to him.

 **17** ## August 12, 1909

We were in the Kikuyu country. On our march we met several parties of natives. I had been much inclined to pity the porters, who had but one blanket apiece; but when I saw the Kikuyus, each with nothing but a smaller blanket, and without the other clothing and the tents of the porters, I realized how much better off the latter were simply because they were on a white man's safari. At Nyeri boma we were greeted with the warmest hospitality by the district commissioner, Mr. Browne. Among other things, he arranged a great Kikuyu dance in our honor. Two thousand warriors, and many women, came in; as well as a small party of Maasai moran [young warriors]. The warriors were naked, or half-naked; some carried gaudy blankets, others girdles of leopard skin; their ox-hide shields were colored in bold patterns, their long-bladed spears quivered and gleamed. Their faces and legs were painted red and yellow; the faces of the young men who were about to undergo the rite of circumcision were

Unidentified photographer, *Native Dance Held at Nyeri in Father's Honor*, August 12, 1909

Left: Unidentified photographer, *Native Dance Held at Nyeri in Father's Honor*, August 12, 1909
Next page: Unidentified photographer, *Native Dance Held at Nyeri in Father's Honor*, August 12, 1909

stained a ghastly white, and their bodies fantastically painted. The warriors wore bead necklaces and waist belts and armlets of brass and steel, and spurred anklets of monkey skin. Some wore head-dresses made out of a lion's mane or from the long black and white fur of the Colobus monkey; others had plumes stuck in their red-daubed hair. They chanted in unison a deep-toned chorus, and danced rhythmically in rings, while the drums throbbed, and the horns blared; and they danced by us in column, springing and chanting. The women shrilled applause and danced in groups by themselves. The Maasai circled and swung in a panther-like dance of their own, and the measure, and their own fierce singing and calling, maddened them until two of their number, their eyes staring, their faces working, went into fits, of berserker frenzy, and were disarmed at once to prevent mischief. Some of the tribesmen held wilder dances still in the evening, by the light of fires that blazed in a grove where their thatched huts stood.

Unidentified photographer, *Kikuyu Woman at Nyeri*, August 1909

Climbing Mount Kenya

Three distinct tribes—the Kikuyu, Embu, and Meru—inhabit the area surrounding Mount Kenya. Each regards it as a sacred place. For the Kikuyu, the largest of the three groups, the mountain is the home of Ngai, the supreme deity in their cosmology. As ancestral spirits also reside there, many spiritual and cultural practices occur at or refer to the mountain.

For European travelers, Mount Kenya has long been of great scientific interest. In the 1880s, they first began to survey the mountain, with a particular interest in its flora and fauna. Trekking toward its summit was never something that Roosevelt prepared for nor envisioned doing then. Yet for the three Smithsonian naturalists, exploring the mountain was regarded as one of the expedition's highlights. While Roosevelt went out in search of elephants with Cuninghame and Heller on the lower plains, Mearns and Loring—and later Heller—made a thorough biological survey of the mountain. During their trek they took copious notes about the alpine environment. Changes that occurred at different elevations fascinated them, and Heller and Loring created numerous photographs of the plants and wildlife they encountered. Having climbed to 14,500 feet, they passed glacial lakes and had a dramatic view of the snow-covered peaks of the mountain.

18   Late August 1909

The second day after reaching Nyeri the clouds lifted and we dried our damp clothes and blankets. Through the bright sunlight we saw in front of us the high rock peaks of Kenya, and shining among them the fields of everlasting snow which feed her glaciers; for beautiful, lofty Kenya is one of the glacier-bearing mountains of the equator. Here Kermit and Tarlton went northward on a safari of their own, while Cuninghame, Heller, and I headed for Kenya itself. For two days we travelled through a well-peopled country. The fields of corn—always called mealies in Africa—of beans, and sweet-potatoes, with occasional plantations of bananas, touched one another in almost uninterrupted succession. In most of them we saw the Kikuyu women at work with their native hoes; for among the Kikuyus, as among other savages, the woman is the drudge and beast of burden. Our trail led by clear, rushing streams, which

Edmund Heller, *Giant Groundsel on Alpine Moors of Kenia*, 1909

Edmund Heller, *Clouds on Mount Kenya*, 1909

formed the headwaters of the Tana; among the trees fringing their banks were graceful palms, and there were groves of tree ferns here and there on the sides of the gorges.

On the afternoon of the second day, we struck upward among the steep foothills of the mountain, riven by deep ravines. We pitched camp in an open glade, surrounded by the green wall of tangled forest, the forest of the tropical mountain sides.

The trees, strange of kind and endless in variety, grew tall and close, laced together by vine and creeper, while underbrush crowded the space between their mossy trunks, and covered the leafy mould beneath. Toward dusk crested ibis flew overhead with harsh clamor, to seek their night roosts; parrots chattered, and a curiously home-like touch was given by the presence of a thrush in color and shape almost exactly like our robin. Monkeys called in the depths of the forest, and after dark tree-frogs piped and croaked, and the tree hyraxes uttered their wailing cries.

Edmund Heller, *Glacial Lake on Mount Kenya*, 1909

Elephants dwelt permanently in this mountainous region of heavy woodland. On our march thither we had already seen their traces in the "shambas," as the cultivated fields of the natives are termed; for the great beasts are fond of raiding the crops at night, and their inroads often do serious damage. In this neighborhood their habit is to live high up in the mountains, in the bamboos, while the weather is dry; the cows and calves keeping closer to the bamboos than the bulls. A spell of wet weather, such as we had fortunately been having, drives them down in the dense forest which covers the lower slopes. Here they may either pass all their time, or at night they may go still further down, into the open valley where the shambas lie; or they may occasionally still do what they habitually did in the days before the white hunters came, and wander far away, making migrations that are sometimes seasonal, and sometimes irregular and unaccountable.

Hunting Elephants

Throughout the safari Roosevelt received mail and telegrams that allowed him to keep up with family and friends and to learn about noteworthy happenings. Although he professed a desire to remain at arm's length from political news occurring back in Washington, he was interested in stories that were then making headlines. Of special interest was the progress of explorer Robert E. Peary, who had embarked during the previous summer on his eighth trip into the Arctic. Peary's goal was to be the first man to reach the North Pole, a feat that had eluded him for more than two decades. Roosevelt had been on hand at Peary's departure from Long Island, as he set sail aboard the SS *Roosevelt*, a boat that Peary designed himself to withstand the dangerous Arctic ice and named in honor of his friend.

On September 12, while hunting near Meru on the northeastern slope of Mount Kenya, Roosevelt received a cable, forwarded by African runners, describing a recent report that Peary, his colleague Matthew Henson, and four Inuit assistants had reached the North Pole in April. The news delighted him. Yet, the message also indicated that Peary's rival Frederick A. Cook was then proclaiming that he had reached the Pole too and had done so a year before Peary. Roosevelt was skeptical of Cook's claim and angered by the controversy. In a letter to his sister Anna Cowles, he expressed his admiration of Peary and his disdain for Cook: "That Peary reached the pole I am sure; whether or not Cook did I can't say, for Cook, though a capable man, is a fake." Other letters from East Africa suggest that the controversy continued to occupy his mind throughout the fall.

While the Smithsonian naturalists surveyed Mount Kenya, the Roosevelts focused their attention on elephants, the last of the large mammals they had yet to kill. Accompanied by Cuninghame and local Ndorobo hunting guides, they went in search of a suite of specimens that they could add to their collection. For several weeks this hunt occupied their attention.

19 Early September 1909

No other animal, not the lion himself, is so constant a theme of talk, and a subject of such unflagging interest round the campfires of African hunters and in the native villages of the African wilderness as the elephant. Indeed, the elephant has always profoundly impressed the imagination

R. J. Cuninghame, *The First Bull Elephant*, 1909

of mankind. It is, not only to hunters, but to naturalists, and to all people who possess any curiosity about wild creatures and the wildlife of nature, the most interesting of all animals. Its huge bulk, its singular form, the value of its ivory, its great intelligence—in which it is only matched, if at all, by the highest apes, and possibly by one or two of the highest carnivores—and its varied habits, all combine to give it an interest such as attaches to no other living creature below the rank of man. In line of descent and in physical formation it stands by itself, wholly apart from all the other great land beasts, and differing from them even more widely than they differ from one another. The two existing species—the African, which is the larger and finer animal, and the Asiatic—differ from one another as much as they do from the mammoth and similar extinct forms which were the contemporaries of early man in Europe and North America. The carvings of our palaeolithic forefathers, etched on bone by cavern dwellers, from whom we are sundered by ages which stretch into an immemorial past, show that in their lives the hairy elephant of the north played the same part that his remote collateral descendant now plays in the lives of the savages who dwell under a vertical sun beside the tepid waters of the Nile and the Congo. . . .

The elephant is unique among the beasts of great bulk in the fact that his growth in size has been accompanied by growth in brain power. With other beasts growth in bulk of body has not been accompanied by similar growth of mind. Indeed, sometimes there seems to have been mental retrogression. The rhinoceros, in several different forms, is found in the same regions as the elephant, and in one of its forms it is in point of size second only to the elephant among terrestrial animals. Seemingly the ancestors of the two creatures, in that period, separated from us by uncounted hundreds of thousands of years, which we may conveniently designate as late miocene or early pliocene, were substantially equal in brain development. But in one case increase in bulk seems to have induced lethargy and atrophy of brain power, while in the other case brain and body have both grown. At any rate the elephant is now one of the wisest and the rhinoceros one of the stupidest of big mammals. In consequence the elephant outlasts the rhino, although he is the largest, carries infinitely more valuable spoils, and is far more eagerly and persistently hunted. Both animals wandered freely over the open country of East Africa thirty years ago. But the elephant learns by experience infinitely more readily than the rhinoceros. As a rule, the former no longer live in the open plains, and in many places now even cross them if possible only at night. But those rhinoceros which formerly dwelt in the plains for the most part continued to dwell there until killed out. So it is at the present day. Not the most foolish elephant would under similar conditions behave as the rhinos that we studied and hunted by Kilimakiu and in the Sotik behaved. No elephant, in regions where they have been much persecuted by hunters, would habitually spend its days lying or standing in the open plain; nor would it, in such places, repeatedly, and in fact uniformly, permit men to walk boldly up to it without heeding them until in its immediate neighborhood. The elephant's sight is bad, as is that of the rhinoceros; but a comparatively brief experience with rifle-bearing man usually makes the former take refuge in regions where scent and hearing count for more than sight, while no experience has any such effect on the rhino. The rhinos that now live in the bush are the descendants of those which always lived in the bush; and it is in the bush that the species will linger long after it has vanished from the open; and it is in the bush that it is most formidable.

Elephant and rhino differ as much in their habits as in their intelligence. The former is very gregarious, herds of several hundred being sometimes found, and is of a restless, wandering temper, often shifting his abode and sometimes making long migrations. The rhinoceros is a lover of solitude; it is usually found alone, or a bull and cow, or cow and calf may be in company; very rarely are as many as half a dozen found together. Moreover, it is comparatively stationary in its habits, and as a general thing stays permanently in one neighborhood, not shifting its position for very many miles unless for grave reasons.

Next Page: Unidentified photographer, *Ndorobo Elephant Guides, 1st Camp*, 1909

Edmund Heller, *Camping after Death of the First Bull*, 1909

The African elephant has recently been divided into a number of sub-species; but as within a century its range was continuous over nearly the whole continent south of the Sahara, and as it was given to such extensive occasional wanderings, it is probable that the examination of a sufficient series of specimens would show that on their confines these races grade into one another. In its essentials the beast is almost everywhere the same, although, of course, there must be variation of habits with any animal which exists throughout so wide and diversified a range of territory; for in one place it is found in high mountains, in another in a dry desert, in another in low-lying marshes or wet and dense forests.

In East Africa the old bulls are usually found singly or in small parties by themselves. These have the biggest tusks; the bulls in the prime of life, the herd bulls or breeding bulls, which keep in herds with the cows and calves, usually have smaller ivory. Sometimes, however, very old but vigorous bulls are found with the cows; and I am inclined to think that the ordinary herd bulls at times also keep by themselves, or at least in company with only a few cows, for at certain seasons, generally immediately after the rains, cows, most of them with calves, appear in great numbers at certain places, where only a few bulls are ever found. Where undisturbed elephants rest and wander about at all times of the day and night, and feed without much regard to fixed hours. Morning or evening, noon or midnight, the herd may be on the move, or its members may be resting; yet, during the hottest hours of noon they seldom feed, and ordinarily stand almost still, resting—for elephants very rarely lie down unless sick. Where they are afraid of man, their only enemy, they come out to feed in thinly forested plains, or cultivated fields, when they do so at all, only at night, and before daybreak move back into the forest to rest. Elsewhere they sometimes spend the day in the open, in grass or low bush. Where we were, at this time, on Kenya, the elephants sometimes moved down at night to feed in the shambas, at the expense of the crops of the natives, and sometimes stayed in the forest, feeding by day or night on the branches they tore off the trees, or, occasionally, on the roots they grubbed up with their tusks. They work vast havoc among the young or small growth of a forest, and the readiness with which they uproot, overturn, or break off medium-sized trees conveys a striking impression of their enormous strength. I have seen a tree a foot in diameter thus uprooted and overturned.

The African elephant has never, like his Indian kinsman, been trained to man's use. There is still hope that the feat may be performed; but hitherto its probable economic usefulness has for various reasons seemed so questionable that there has been scant encouragement to undergo the necessary expense and labor. Up to the present time the African elephant has yielded only his ivory as an asset of value. This, however, has been of such great value as wellnigh to bring about the mighty beast's utter extermination. Ivory hunters and ivory traders have penetrated Africa to the haunts of the elephant since centuries before our era, and the elephant's boundaries have been slowly receding throughout historic time; but during the century just past its process has been immensely accelerated, until now there are but one or two out-of-the-way nooks of the Dark Continent to the neighborhood of which hunter and trader have not penetrated. Fortunately, the civilized powers which now divide dominion over Africa have woken up in time, and there is at present no danger of the extermination of the lord of all four-footed creatures. Large reserves have been established on which various herds of elephants now live what is, at least for the time being, an entirely safe life. Furthermore, over great tracts of territory outside the reserves regulations have been promulgated which, if enforced as they are now enforced, will prevent any excessive diminution of the herds. In British East Africa, for instance, no cows are allowed to be shot save for special purposes, as for preservation in a museum, or to safeguard life and property; and no bulls with tusks weighing less than thirty pounds apiece. This renders safe almost all the females and an ample supply of breeding males. Too much praise cannot be given the governments and the individuals who have brought about this happy result; the credit belongs especially to England and to various Englishmen. It would be a veritable and most tragic calamity if the lordly elephant, the giant among existing four-footed creatures, should be permitted to vanish from the face of the earth.

Next page: Kermit Roosevelt, *A Herd of Elephant in an Open Forest of High Timber*, 1909

163

African Guides and Attendants

Having successfully hunted elephants together, the Roosevelts again separated in late September. From their camp in Meru, northeast of Mount Kenya, Kermit started on September 21 west toward Lake Borgoria with Leslie Tarlton. The former president began with Cuninghame northward toward the plains near the Ewaso Ngiro River. They traveled apart for a month before reuniting again in Nairobi. Meanwhile, the Smithsonian naturalists returned to their work on Mount Kenya. During this time Kermit celebrated his twentieth birthday, an occasion that prompted Roosevelt in a letter to his sister Anna Cowles to admit that Kermit "is now a better hunter than I am, for Twenty is hardier and more active and endowed with better eyes than Fifty-One."

The wildlife in East Africa continued to fascinate him, though, as a longtime political leader, he was also intrigued by this region's present and future. He had grown fond of his traveling companions—both the American and British guides and the African attendants who supported the safari—and he frequently pondered the larger issues that they faced. As journalist Francis Dawson wrote at the time, "the two questions which seemed to appeal most to him were the conditions of this new country growing up very much as our own West had done a quarter of a century before, and the conditions of the black man in his primeval state." He described the people in his company with affection, though from his privileged position, he also understood them as servants and at times subjects in a larger scientific study.

 20 **September 21 to October 20, 1909**

I had kept four Kikuyus with me to accompany me on my hunts and carry in the skins and meat. They were with me on this occasion; and it was amusing to see how my four regular attendants, Bakhari and Gouvimali the gunbearers, Simba the sais, and Kiboko the skinner, looked down on their wild and totally uncivilized brethren. They would not associate with the "shenzis," as they called them; that is, savages or bush people. But the "shenzis" always amused and interested me; and this was especially true on the afternoon in question. Soon after we had started campwards with the skin and meat of the oryx, we encountered a succession of thunderstorms. The rain came down in a deluge, so that the water stood ankle deep on the flats, the lightning flashed continuously on every side, and the terrific peals of thunder made one continuous roll. At first it maddened my horse; but the uninterrupted blaze and roar, just because uninterrupted, ended

Theodore Roosevelt, *My Boma When I Was Camped Alone*, 1909

by making him feel that there was nothing to be done, and he plodded stolidly forward through the driving storm. My regular attendants accepted it with an entire philosophy, which was finally copied by the Kikuyus, who at first felt frightened. One of them had an old umbrella which he shared with a crony. He himself was carrying the marabou stork; his crony had long strips of raw oryx meat wound in a swollen girdle about his waist; neither had a stitch on save the blankets which were wrapped round their throats; and they clasped each other in a tight embrace as they walked along under the battered old umbrella.

In this desolate and lonely land, the majesty of the storms impressed on the beholder a sense of awe and solemn exaltation. Tossing their crests, and riven by lightning, they gathered in their wrath from every quarter of the heavens, and darkness was before and under them; then, in the lull of a moment, they might break apart, while the sun turned the rain to silver and the rainbows were set in the sky; but always they gathered again, menacing and mighty,—for the promise of the bow was never kept, and ever the clouds returned after the rain. Once as I rode facing Kenya the clouds tore asunder, to right and left, and the mountain towered between, while across its base was flung a radiant arch. But almost at once the many-colored glory was dimmed; for in splendor and terror the storm strode in front and shrouded all things from sight in thunder-shattered sheets of rain.

These days alone in the wilderness went by very pleasantly, and, as it was for not too long, I thoroughly enjoyed being entirely by myself, so far as white men were concerned. By this time, I had become really attached to my native followers, who looked after my interest and comfort in every way; and in return I kept them supplied with plenty of food, saw that they were well clothed, and forced them to gather enough firewood to keep their tents dry and warm at night— for cold, rainy weather is always hard upon them.

Ali, my faithful head tent boy, and Shemlani his assistant—poor Bill the Kikuyu had left because of an intricate row with his fellows—were both, as they proudly informed me, Arabs. On the East African coast the so-called Arabs almost all have native blood in them and speak Swahili; the curious, newly created language of the descendants of the natives whom the Arabs originally enslaved, and who themselves may have in their veins a little Arab blood; in fact, the dividing line between Swahili and Arab becomes impracticable for an outsider to draw where, as is generally the case, it is patent that the blood of both races is mixed to a degree at which it is only possible to guess. Ali spoke some English; and he and Shemlani were devoted and efficient servitors. Bakhari the gunbearer was a Swahili, quite fearless with dangerous game, rather sullen, and unmoved by any emotion that I could ever discover. He spoke a little English, but it could not be called idiomatic. One day we saw two ostriches, a cock and a hen, with their chicks, and Bakhari with some excitement said, "Look, sah! ostrich! bull, cow, and pups!" The other gun-bearer, Gouvimali, in some ways an even better hunter, and always good-tempered, knew but one English phrase; regularly every afternoon or evening, after cleaning the

Theodore Roosevelt, *Ivory-Nut Palms on the Guaso Nyero*, 1909

Next page: Unidentified photographer, *Bibi Porters, Nyeri*, 1909

Kermit Roosevelt, *Juma Yohari with Nilotic Bushbuck*, December 1909

rifle he had carried, he would say, as he left the tent, his face wreathed in smiles, "G-o-o-d-e-bye!" Gouvimali was a Wakamba, as were Simba and my other sais, M'nyassa, who had taken the place of Hamisi (Hamisi had broken down in health, his legs, as he assured me, becoming "very sick"). The cook, Roberti, was a mission boy, a Christian; we had several Christians with the safari, one being a headman, and all did excellently. I mention this because one so often hears it said that mission boys turn out worthless. Most of our men were heathens; and of course, many, both of the Christians and the Mohammedans, were rather thinly veneered with the religions they respectively professed.

When in the morning we started on our hunt my gunbearers and sais, and the skinners, if any were along, walked silently behind me, on the lookout for game. Returning, they were apt to get in front, to pilot me back to camp. If, as at this time was generally the case, we returned with our heads bent to the rushing rain, they trudged sturdily ahead in dripping silence. If the weather was clear the spirits of the stalwart fellows were sure to rise until they found some expression. The Wakamba might break into song; or they might all talk together in Swahili, recounting the adventures of the day, and chaffing one another with uproarious laughter about any small misadventure; a difference of opinion as to the direction of camp being always a subject, first for earnest discussion, and then for much mirth at the expense of whomever the event proved mistaken.

Edmund Heller, *A Watchtower in Meru Shambas*, September 1909

Leopards

The collecting and documenting of specimens continued apace throughout the fall. Preparing these items for shipment to Washington was a specialized and time-consuming task led by the Smithsonian naturalists with the invaluable help of their African assistants. Each item had to be measured, catalogued, and preserved; many items were also photographed at the time of their collection, and details about their habitats, behavior in the field, eating habits, and markings recorded. Some were simply placed in a padded box upon being collected, whereas others required teams of people and days of preparation before they could be shipped. Skinning parties of a dozen or more individuals were often organized to handle large mammals. As a preservation agent, salt was essential in this process, and the expedition consumed large quantities. Once ready for shipment, the crated items were transported by a team of porters to Nairobi, where Newland, Tarlton & Company received and stored them before the next phase of their trip to the United States.

Although he was primarily a hunter, Roosevelt appreciated the expertise and labor that went into the preparation of the safari's collected specimens. He understood that the proper display and future research related to these items depended on this fieldwork. In his writings he spoke often about collecting only those animals that would be of future scientific value. Yet he also hunted for other reasons, including to feed the safari and to protect themselves and others from predatory animals. Though many animals might attack if provoked, lions and leopards were especially feared because of their reputation for hunting humans. Stories abounded about these encounters, and safari members assisted at times in the effort to eliminate animals regarded as problematic.

 **October 1909**

During our stay another district commissioner, Mr. Piggott, came over on a short visit; it was he who the preceding year, while at Nyeri, had been obliged to undertake the crusade against the rhinos, because, quite unprovoked, they had killed various natives. He told us that at the same time a man-eating leopard made its appearance and killed seven children. It did not attack at night, but in the daytime, its victims being the little boys who were watching the flocks of goats; sometimes it took a boy and sometimes a goat. Two old men killed it with spears on the occasion of its taking the last victim. It was a big male, very old, much

174

Paul Thompson, *Kermit Roosevelt Photographing a Porcupine from Above*, 1909

Next page: Unidentified photographer, *Camp Skinning Bee*, 1909

emaciated, and the teeth worn to stumps. Horne told us that a month or two before our arrival at Meru a leopard had begun a career of woman-killing. It killed one woman by a bite in the throat and ate the body. It sprang on and badly wounded another but was driven off in time to save her life. This was probably the leopard Heller trapped and shot, in the very locality where it had committed its ravages; it was an old male, but very thin, with worn teeth. In these cases, the reason for the beast's action was plain: in each instance a big, savage male had found his powers failing, and had been driven to prey on the females and young of the most helpless of animals, man. But another attack, of which Piggott told us, was apparently due to the queer individual freakishness always to be taken into account in dealing with wild beasts. A Maasai chief, with two or three followers, was sitting eating under a bush, when, absolutely without warning, a leopard sprang on him, clawed him on the head and hand, without biting him, and as instantly disappeared. Piggott attended to the wounded man.

Unidentified photographer, *African Holds Dead Leopard*, 1909

Toward Mount Elgon and Hunting with Carl Akeley

After a month apart, the safari members reunited once again in Nairobi in mid-October. Their time there was short, for they ventured out again into the field several days later. They took the railway northwest to Londiani, where they disembarked and moved overland toward Mount Elgon, an extinct volcano more than 14,000 feet tall on the border of present-day Kenya and Uganda, traversing the Uasin Gishu plateau and the Nzoia River on the way.

While in Nairobi, Roosevelt crossed paths with James L. Clark from the American Museum of Natural History and learned that Carl Akeley was due to arrive in Nairobi shortly. The acclaimed naturalist had traveled there to join Clark's expedition but was also interested in spending some time with Roosevelt. Though each had their own expedition for which they were responsible, Roosevelt invited Akeley for a short visit. On November 14 the two met on the Uasin Gishu plateau and spent the next two days hunting elephants. Of the reunion Akeley later wrote, "We all went back to our camp for luncheon, where I gave Roosevelt a bottle of very choice brandy, a present from Mr. Oscar Strauss. Mr. Strauss had been one of our steamer companions across the Atlantic and, learning that I was likely to meet Roosevelt, he asked me to take this choice brandy to him in the jungles. Roosevelt accepted it with much interest in the accompanying message but apparently with mighty little interest in the brandy. He passed the bottle on to Cuninghame and I felt certain it would eventually meet with just appreciation." Their time together was short, though memorable.

 22 **October 21 to November 16, 1909**

After leaving the elephants we were on our way back to camp when we saw a white man in the trail ahead; and on coming nearer whom should it prove to be but Carl Akeley, who was out on a trip for the American Museum of Natural History in New York. We went with him to his camp, where we found Mrs. Akeley, Clark, who was assisting him, and Messrs. McCutcheon and Stevenson who were along on a hunting trip. They were old friends, and I was very glad to see them. McCutcheon, the cartoonist, had been at a farewell lunch given me by Robert Collier just before I left New York, and at the lunch we had been talking much of George Ade, and the first question I put to him was "*Where* is George Ade?" for if one unexpectedly meets an American cartoonist on a hunting trip in mid-Africa there seems no reason why one should not also see his crony, an American playwright. A year previously Mr. and Mrs. Akeley had lunched with me at the White House, and we had talked over our proposed African trips. Akeley, an old African wanderer, was going out with the especial purpose of getting a group of elephants for the American Museum and was anxious that I should shoot one or two of them for him. I had told him that I certainly would if it were a possibility; and on learning that we had just seen a herd of cows he felt—as I did—that the chance had come for me to fulfil my promise. So we decided that he should camp with us that night, and that next morning we would start with a light outfit to see whether we could not overtake the herd.

An amusing incident occurred that evening. After dark some of the porters went through the reeds to get water from the pond in the middle of the swamp. I was sitting in my tent when a loud yelling and screaming rose from the swamp, and in rushed Kongoni to say that one of the men, while drawing water, had been seized by a lion. Snatching up a rifle I was off at a run for the swamp, calling for lanterns; Kermit and Tarlton joined me, the lanterns were brought, and we reached the meadow of short marsh grass which surrounded the high reeds in the middle. No sooner were we on this meadow than there were loud snortings in the darkness ahead of us, and then the sound of a heavy animal galloping across our front. It now developed that there was no lion in the case at all, but that the porters had been chased by a hippo. I should not have supposed that a hippo would live in such a small, isolated swamp; but there he was on the meadow in front of me, invisible, but snorting, and galloping to and fro. Evidently, he was much interested in the lights, and we thought he might charge us; but he did not, retreating slowly as we advanced, until he plunged into the little pond. Hippos are sometimes dangerous at night, and so we waded through the swamp until we came to the pool at which the porters filled their buckets and stood guard over them until they were through; while the hippo, unseen in the darkness, came closer to us, snorting and plunging—possibly from wrath and insolence, but more probably from mere curiosity.

Next morning Akeley, Tarlton, Kermit, and I started on our elephant hunt. We were travelling light. I took nothing but my bedding, wash kit, spare socks, and slippers, all in a roll of waterproof canvas. We went to where we had seen the herd and then took up the trail, Kongoni and two or three other gun-bearers walking ahead as trackers. They did their work well. The elephants had not been in the least alarmed. Where they had walked in single file it was easy to follow their trail; but the trackers had hard work puzzling it out where the animals had scattered out and loitered along feeding. The trail led up and down hills and through open thorn scrub, and it crossed and recrossed the wooded watercourses in the bottoms of the valleys. At last, after going some ten miles we came on sign where the elephants had fed that morning, and four or five miles further on we overtook them. That we did not scare them into flight was due to Tarlton. The trail went nearly across wind; the trackers were leading us swiftly along it, when suddenly Tarlton heard a low trumpet ahead and to the right hand. We at once doubled back, left the horses, and advanced toward where the noise indicated that the herd was standing.

Leslie Tarlton, *Carl Akeley, Kermit Roosevelt, and Theodore Roosevelt with a Dead Elephant*, November 15, 1909

In a couple of minutes, we sighted them. It was just noon. There were six cows, and two well-grown calves—these last being quite big enough to shift for themselves or to be awkward antagonists for any man of whom they could get hold. They stood in a clump, each occasionally shifting its position or lazily flapping an ear; and now and then one would break off a branch with its trunk, tuck it into its mouth, and withdraw it stripped of its leaves. The wind blew fair, we were careful to make no noise, and with ordinary caution we had nothing to fear from their eyesight. The ground was neither forest nor bare plain; it was covered with long grass and a scattered open growth of small, scantily leaved trees, chiefly mimosas, but including some trees covered with gorgeous orange-red flowers. After careful scrutiny we advanced behind an anthill to within sixty yards, and I stepped forward for the shot.

Akeley wished two cows and a calf. Of the two best cows one had rather thick, worn tusks; those of the other were smaller, but better shaped. The latter stood half facing me, and I put the bullet from the right barrel of the Holland through her lungs and fired the left barrel for the heart of the other.

Kermit Roosevelt, *Beginning to Work on the Skin*, November 1909

Tarlton, and then Akeley and Kermit, followed suit. At once the herd started diagonally past us, but half halted and faced toward us when only twenty-five yards distant, an unwounded cow beginning to advance with her great ears cocked at right angles to her head; and Tarlton called "Look out; they are coming for us." At such a distance a charge from half a dozen elephants is a serious thing; I put a bullet into the forehead of the advancing cow, causing her to lurch heavily forward to her knees; and then we all fired. The heavy rifles were too much even for such big beasts, and round they spun and rushed off. As they turned, I dropped the second cow I had wounded with a shot in the brain, and the cow that had started to charge also fell, though it needed two or three more shots to keep it down as it struggled to rise. The cow at which I had first fired kept on with the rest of the herd but fell dead before going a hundred yards. After we had turned the herd Kermit with his Winchester killed a bull calf, necessary to complete the museum group; we had been unable to kill it before because we were too busy stopping the charge of the cows. I was sorry to have to shoot the third cow, but with elephant starting to charge at twenty-five yards the risk is too great, and the need of instant action too imperative, to allow of any hesitation.

Carl Akeley, *Theodore Roosevelt Taking a Photograph of a Hyena Trapped in a Skinned Elephant,*
November 16, 1909

We pitched camp a hundred yards from the elephants, and Akeley, working like a demon, and
assisted by Tarlton, had the skins off the two biggest cows and the calf by the time night fell; I walked
out and shot an oribi for supper. Soon after dark the hyenas began to gather at the carcasses and to
quarrel among themselves as they gorged. Toward morning a lion came near and uttered a kind
of booming, long-drawn moan, an ominous and menacing sound. The hyenas answered with an
extraordinary chorus of yelling, howling, laughing, and chuckling, as weird a volume of noise as any
to which I ever listened. At dawn we stole down to the carcasses in the faint hope of a shot at the lion.
However, he was not there; but as we came toward one carcass a hyena raised its head seemingly from
beside the elephant's belly, and I brained it with the little Springfield. On walking up, it appeared that
I need not have shot at all. The hyena, which was swollen with elephant meat, had gotten inside the
huge body, and had then bitten a hole through the abdominal wall of tough muscle and thrust his
head through. The wedge-shaped head had slipped through the hole all right, but the muscle had
then contracted, and the hyena was fairly caught, with its body inside the elephant's belly, and its head
thrust out through the hole. We took several photos of the beast in its queer trap.

Lion Hunt with the Nandi

Akeley and Roosevelt went separate directions after three days together. In his later recollections of the expedition, Akeley indicated that he had been especially interested in filming a lion hunt: "However, I found that you can't stage a native lion hunt without any certainty, for neither the lion nor the native, once the action begins, pays any attention to the movie director. In order to have even a fair chance of following the action with a camera you need one that you can aim up, down, and in any direction with about the same ease that you can point a pistol. There were no movie cameras like this, and after failing to get pictures of several lions I determined not to go to Africa again until I had one."

Roosevelt had earlier hunted for lions, but he had yet to experience a hunt without guns. Two days after departing from Akeley, he had the opportunity to witness one among the Nandi. A tribal community in the region of Mount Elgon, the Nandi, under the military and spiritual leadership of Koitalel Arap Samoei, had actively resisted outside encroachments since the 1890s. They had no interest in the Uganda Railway and British settlement on their homelands. In 1905, British authorities controversially killed Koitalel during a peace meeting. Shortly thereafter, a truce was negotiated, and the Nandi became part of the British East Africa Protectorate. Roosevelt alludes to these recent events but fails to explore them.

23 November 17 to December 10, 1909

The Nandi are a warlike pastoral tribe, close kin to the Maasai in blood and tongue, in weapons and in manner of life. They have long been accustomed to kill with the spear lions which become man-eaters or which molest their cattle overmuch; and the peace which British rule has imposed upon them—a peace so welcome to the weaker, so irksome to the predatory, tribes—has left lion killing one of the few pursuits in which glory can be won by a young warrior. When it was told them that if they wished they could come to hunt lions at Sergoi eight hundred warriors volunteered, and much heart-burning was caused in choosing the sixty or seventy who were allowed the privilege. They stipulated, however, that they should not be used merely as beaters, but should kill the lion themselves, and refused to come unless with this understanding.

The day before we reached Sergoi they had gone out and had killed a lion and lioness; the beasts were put up from a small covert and despatched with the heavy throwing spears on the instant, before they offered, or indeed had the chance to offer, any resistance. The day after our arrival there was mist and cold rain, and we found no lions. Next day, November 20th, we were successful.

We started immediately after breakfast. Kirke, Skally, Mouton, Jordaan, Mr. and Mrs. Corbett, Captain Chapman, and our party, were on horseback; of course we carried our rifles, but our duty was merely to round up the lion and hold him, if he went off so far in advance that even the Nandi runners could not overtake him. We intended to beat the country toward some shallow, swampy valleys twelve miles distant.

In an hour we overtook the Nandi warriors, who were advancing across the rolling, grassy plains in a long line, with intervals of six or eight yards between the men. They were splendid savages, stark naked, lithe as panthers, the muscles rippling under their smooth dark skins; all their lives they had lived on nothing but animal food, milk, blood, and flesh, and they were fit for any fatigue or danger. Their faces were proud, cruel, fearless; as they ran they moved with long springy strides. Their headdresses were fantastic; they carried ox-hide shields painted with strange devices; and each bore in his right hand the formidable war spear, used both for stabbing and for throwing at close quarters. The narrow spear heads of soft iron were burnished till they shone like silver; they were four feet long, and the point and edges were razor sharp. The wooden haft appeared for but a few inches; the long butt was also of iron, ending in a spike, so that the spear looked almost solid metal. Yet each sinewy warrior carried his heavy weapon as if it were a toy, twirling it till it glinted in the sunrays. Herds of game, red hartebeests and striped zebra and wild swine, fled right and left before the advance of the line.

It was noon before we reached a wide, shallow valley, with beds of rushes here and there in the middle, and on either side high grass and dwarfed and scattered thorn-trees. Down this we beat for a couple of miles. Then, suddenly, a maned lion rose a quarter of a mile ahead of the line and galloped off through the high grass to the right; and all of us on horseback tore after him. He was a magnificent beast, with a black and tawny mane; in his prime, teeth and claws perfect, with mighty thews, and savage heart. He was lying near a hartebeest on which he had been feasting; his life had been one unbroken career of rapine and violence; and now the maned master of the wilderness, the terror that stalked by night, the grim lord of slaughter, was to meet his doom at the hands of the only foes who dared molest him.

It was a mile before we brought him to bay. Then the Dutch farmer, Mouton, who had not even a rifle, but who rode foremost, was almost on him; he halted and turned under a low thorn-tree, and we galloped past him to the opposite side, to hold him until the spearmen could come. It was a sore temptation to shoot him; but of course, we could not break faith with our Nandi friends.

Leslie Tarlton, *Member of the Safari Party with a Camera Standing over a Lion Killed with Spears,*
November 20, 1909

We were only some sixty yards from him, and we watched him with our rifles ready, lest he should charge either of us, or the first two or three spearmen, before their companions arrived.

One by one the spearmen came up, at a run, and gradually began to form a ring round him. Each, when he came near enough, crouched behind his shield, his spear in his right hand, his fierce, eager face peering over the shield rim. As man followed man, the lion rose to his feet. His mane bristled, his tail lashed, he held his head low, the upper lip now drooping over the jaws, now drawn up so as to show the gleam of the long fangs. He faced first one way and then another, and never ceased to utter his murderous grunting roars. It was a wild sight; the ring of spearmen, intent, silent, bent on blood, and in the center the great man-killing beast, his thunderous wrath growing ever more dangerous.

Next page: Edmund Heller, *Nandi Lion Hunt*, November 1909

Edmund Heller, *Nandi Warriors Dancing after Killing a Lion with Spears. Theodore Roosevelt is Taking a Photograph of the Warriors*, November 20, 1909

At last, the tense ring was complete, and the spearmen rose and closed in. The lion looked quickly from side to side, saw where the line was thinnest, and charged at his topmost speed. The crowded moment began. With shields held steady, and quivering spears poised, the men in front braced themselves for the rush and the shock; and from either hand the warriors sprang forward to take their foe in flank. Bounding ahead of his fellows, the leader reached throwing distance; the long spear flickered and plunged; as the lion felt the wound he half turned, and then flung himself on the man in front. The warrior threw his spear; it drove deep into the life, for entering at one shoulder it came out of the opposite flank, near the thigh, a yard of steel through the great body. Rearing, the lion struck the man, bearing down the shield, his back arched; and for a moment he slaked his fury with fang and talon. But on the instant, I saw another spear driven clear through his body from side to side; and as the lion turned again the bright spear blades darting toward him were flashes of white flame. The end had come. He seized another man, who stabbed him and wrenched loose. As he fell, he gripped a spearhead in his jaws with such tremendous force that he bent it double. Then the warriors were round and over him, stabbing and shouting, wild with furious exultation.

From the moment when he charged until his death, I doubt whether ten seconds had elapsed, perhaps less; but what a ten seconds! The first half-dozen spears had done the work. Three of the

Unidentified photographer, *After the Lion Spearing*, November 20, 1909

spear blades had gone clear through the body, the points projecting several inches; and these, and one or two others, including the one he had seized in his jaws, had been twisted out of shape in the terrible death struggle.

We at once attended to the two wounded men. Treating their wounds with antiseptic was painful, and so, while the operation was in progress, I told them, through Kirke, that I would give each a heifer. A Nandi prizes his cattle rather more than his wives; and each sufferer smiled broadly at the news and forgot all about the pain of his wounds.

Then the warriors, raising their shields above their heads, and chanting the deep-toned victory song, marched with a slow, dancing step around the dead body of the lion; and this savage dance of triumph ended a scene of as fierce interest and excitement as I ever hope to see.

The Nandi marched back by themselves, carrying the two wounded men on their shields. We rode to camp by a roundabout way, on the chance that we might see another lion. The afternoon waned and we cast long shadows before us as we rode across the vast lonely plain. The game stared at us as we passed; a cold wind blew in our faces, and the tall grass waved ceaselessly; the sun set behind a sullen cloud bank; and then, just at nightfall, the tents glimmered white through the dusk.

Visit with Lord Delamere and Hunting Bongo with the Ndorobo

Following the lion hunt, Edmund Heller returned again to Nairobi to oversee the next shipment of specimens. Meanwhile, the Roosevelts traveled to visit Hugh Cholmondeley, the Third Baron Delamere, at his ranch outside Njoro. Lord Delamere was one of the earliest and most influential British settlers in East Africa. Since 1904 he had served as the president of the Colonial Association, an organization that advocated for the development of farming and ranching in the region. Over the next three decades, he played an active role in recruiting aristocratic British families to settle there. This group became known as the "Happy Valley" set and gained a wide reputation for its racist beliefs and often hedonistic manners.

Roosevelt spent the first ten days of December with Lord Delamere. Since the safari had planned to travel next into Uganda with a much-reduced entourage, he dismissed most of his African porters at this time. Roosevelt was interested in hunting for bongo, a type of large antelope with twisted horns that he had not yet encountered. Bongo are known for being elusive and, though they frequented the forests near Njoro and though local Ndorobo guides assisted them, the former president was unsuccessful in killing one. On a separate trip with Barclay Cole, Lady Delamere's brother, however, Kermit was successful.

24 Early December 1909

We spent several days vainly hunting bongo in the dense mountain forests, with half a dozen Ndorobo. These were true Ndorobo, who never cultivate the ground, living in the deep forests on wild honey and game. It has been said that they hunt but little, and only elephant and rhino; but this is not correct as regards the Ndorobo in question. They were all clad in short cloaks of the skin of the tree hyrax; hyrax, monkey, bongo, and forest hog, the only game of the dense, cool, wet forest, were all habitually killed by them. They also occasionally killed rhino and buffalo, finding the former, because it must occasionally be attacked in the open, the more dangerous of the two; twice Delamere had come across small communities of Ndorobo literally starving because the strong man, the chief hunter, the breadwinner, had been killed by a rhino which he had attacked. The headman of those

192

with us, who was named Mel-el-lek, had himself been fearfully injured by a wounded buffalo; and the father of another one who was with us had been killed by baboons which had rallied to the aid of one which he was trying to kill with his knobkerry. Usually they did not venture to meddle with the lions which they found on the edge of the forest, or with the leopards which occasionally dwelt in the deep woods; but once Mel-el-lek killed a leopard with a poisoned arrow from a tree, and once a whole party of them attacked and killed with their poisoned arrows a lion which had slain a cow buffalo near the forest. On another occasion a lion in its turn killed two of their hunters. In fact, they were living just as palaeolithic man lived in Europe, ages ago.

Their arms were bows and arrows, the arrows being carried in skin quivers, and the bows, which were strung with zebra gut, being swathed in strips of hide. When resting they often stood on one leg, like storks. Their eyesight was marvelous, and they were extremely skillful alike in tracking and in seeing game. They threaded their way through the forest noiselessly and at speed and were extraordinary climbers. They were continually climbing trees to get at the hyrax, and once when a big black-and-white Colobus monkey which I had shot lodged in the top of a giant cedar one of them ascended and brought it down with matter-of-course indifference. He cut down a sapling, twenty-five feet long, with the stub of a stout branch left on as a hook, and for a rope used a section of vine which he broke and twisted into flexibility. Then, festooned with all his belongings, he made the ascent. There was a tall olive, sixty or eighty feet high, close to the cedar, and up this he went. From its topmost branches, where only a monkey or a Ndorobo could have felt at home, he reached his sapling over to the lowest limb of the giant cedar and hooked it on; and then crawled across on this dizzy bridge. Up he went, got the monkey, recrossed the bridge, and climbed down again, quite unconcerned.

The big black and white monkeys ate nothing but leaves, and usually trusted for safety to ascending into the very tops of the tallest cedars. Occasionally they would come in a flying leap down to the ground, or to a neighboring tree; when on the ground they merely dashed toward another tree, being less agile than the ordinary monkeys, whether in the treetops or on solid earth. They are strikingly handsome and conspicuous creatures. Their bold coloration has been spoken of as "protective"; but it is protective only to town-bred eyes. A non-expert finds any object, of no matter what color, difficult to make out when hidden among the branches at the top of a tall tree; but the black and white coloration of this monkey has not the slightest protective value of any kind. On the contrary, it is calculated at once to attract the eye. The Ndorobo were a unit in saying that these monkeys were much more easy to see than their less brightly colored kinsfolk who dwell in the same forests; and this was my own experience.

When camped in these high forests the woods after nightfall were vocal with the croaking and wailing of the tree hyraxes. They are squat, woolly, funny things, and to my great amusement

Unidentified photographer, *The Ndorobo Hunters Put on Their New Blankets*, December 1909

I found that most of the settlers called them "Teddy bears." They are purely arboreal and nocturnal creatures, living in hollows high up in the big trees, by preference in the cedars. At night they are very noisy, the call consisting of an opening series of batrachian-like croaks, followed by a succession of quavering wails—eerie sounds enough, as they come out of the black stillness of the midnight. They are preyed on now and then by big owls and by leopards, and the white-tailed mongoose is their especial foe, following them everywhere among the treetops. This mongoose is both terrestrial and arboreal in habits and is hated by the Ndorobo because it robs their honey buckets.

The bongo and the giant hog were the big game of these deep forests, where a tangle of undergrowth filled the spaces between the trunks of the cedar, the olive, and the yew or yellow wood, while where the bamboos grew, they usually choked out all other plants. Delamere had killed several giant hogs with his half-breed hounds; but on this occasion the hounds would not follow them. On three days we came across bongo; once a solitary bull, on both the other occasions herds. We never saw them, although we heard the solitary bull crash off through the bamboos; for they are very wary and elusive, being incessantly followed by the Ndorobo. They are as large as native bullocks, with handsomely striped skins, and both sexes carry horns. On each of the three days we followed them all day long, and it was interesting to trace so much as we could of their habits. Their trails are deeply beaten, and converge toward the watercourses, which run between the steep, forest-clad spurs of the mountains. They do not graze, but browse, cropping the leaves, flowers, and twigs of various shrubs, and eating thistles; they are said to eat bark, but this our Ndorobo denied. They are also said to be nocturnal, feeding at night, and lying up in the daytime; but this was certainly not the case with those we came across. Both of the herds, which we followed patiently and cautiously for hours without alarming them, were feeding as they moved slowly along. One herd lay down for a few hours at noon; the other kept feeding until mid-afternoon, when we alarmed it; and the animals then went straight up the mountain over the rimrock. It was cold rainy weather, and the dark of the moon, which may perhaps have had something to do with the bongo being on the move and feeding during the day; but the Ndorobo said that they never fed at night—I of course know nothing about this personally. Leopards catch the young bongo and giant hog but dare not meddle with those that are full-grown. The forest which they frequent is so dense, so well-nigh impenetrable, that half the time no man can follow their trails save by bending and crawling and cannot make out an object twenty yards ahead. It is extraordinary to see the places through which the bongo pass, and which are their chosen haunts.

While Lord Delamere and I were hunting in vain Kermit was more fortunate. He was the guest of Barclay Cole, Delamere's brother-in-law. They took eight porters and went into the forest accompanied by four Ndorobo. They marched straight up to the bamboo and yellow-wood forest near the top of the Mau escarpment. They spent five days hunting. The procedure was simply to find the trail of a herd, to follow it through the tangled woods as rapidly and noiselessly as possible until it was overtaken, and then to try to get a shot at the first patch of reddish hide of which they got a glimpse—for they never saw more than such a patch, and then only for a moment. The first day Kermit, firing at such a patch, knocked over the animal; but it rose, and the tracks were so confused that even the keen eyes of the wild men could not pick out the right one. Next day they again got into a herd; this time Kermit was the first to see the game—all that was visible being a patch of reddish, the size of a man's two hands, with a white stripe across it. Firing he killed the animal; but it proved to be only half grown. Even the Ndorobo now thought it useless to follow the herd; but Kermit took one of them and started in pursuit. After a couple of hours' trailing the herd was again overtaken, and again Kermit got a glimpse of the animals. He hit two; and selecting the trail with most blood they followed it for three or four miles, until Kermit overtook and finished off the wounded bongo, a fine cow. Kermit always found them lying up during the middle of the day and feeding in the morning and afternoon; otherwise, his observations of their habits coincided with mine.

From Nairobi to British Uganda

Roosevelt returned to Nairobi on December 11 and spent a week there being hosted one last time by Governor Jackson and others whom he had gotten to know during his time in East Africa. While there, he learned that a report had recently circulated in the United States about his death—news that naturally alarmed his wife, Edith, and his family. In a letter to his daughter Ethel a day after his arrival, Roosevelt wrote about his commitment to complete his work and the plan to meet in three months at Khartoum: "I am more concerned than I can say about what you tell me as to mother's fright. If this were merely a pleasure trip I should come home at once. But I am the head of a scientific expedition, pledged to do certain work for the Smithsonian, money having been raised on the strength of that pledge. I have advanced the date I am to be at Khartoum all I dare; we will be there by March 15. I couldn't advance it more without upsetting all the work of the three naturalists . . . for the one principle to which I have always adhered in doing any job is to do it just as well as I possibly can."

Following Kermit's return from the coast, where he had been hunting for sable antelope, and one final farewell dinner, the Roosevelts left by train on December 18 headed toward Lake Victoria and Uganda. At the terminus at Kisumu, on the eastern shore of the lake, they disembarked and steamed aboard the SS *Clement Hill* to the port of Entebbe, the headquarters of the British government in Uganda. There and in nearby Kampala, an important economic center, the former president visited local officials, missionaries, and other notables.

 25 **December 11 to 31, 1909**

Kampala is an interesting place; and so is all Uganda. The first explorers who penetrated thither, half a century ago, found in this heathen state, of almost pure negroes, a veritable semi-civilization, or advanced barbarism, comparable to that of the little Arab-negro or Berber-negro sultanates strung along the southern edge of the Sahara, and contrasting sharply with the weltering savagery which surrounded it, and which stretched away without a break for many hundreds of miles in every direction. The people were industrious tillers of the soil, who owned sheep, goats, and some cattle; they wore decent clothing, and hence were styled "womanish" by the savages of the Upper Nile region, who prided themselves on the nakedness of their men as a proof of manliness; they

196

were unusually intelligent and ceremoniously courteous; and, most singular of all, although the monarch was a cruel despot, of the usual African (whether Mohammedan or heathen) type, there were certain excellent governmental customs, of binding observance, which in the aggregate might almost be called an unwritten constitution. Alone among the natives of tropical Africa the people of Uganda have proved very accessible to Christian teaching, so that the creed of Christianity is now dominant among them. For their good fortune, England has established a protectorate over them. Most wisely the English Government officials, and as a rule the missionaries, have bent their energies to developing them along their own lines, in government, dress, and ways of life; constantly striving to better them and bring them forward, but not twisting them aside from their natural line of development, nor wrenching them loose from what was good in their past, by attempting the impossible task of turning an entire native population into black Englishmen at one stroke. . . .

In Africa, the control and guidance are needed as much in the things of the spirit as in the things of the body. Those who complain of or rail at missionary work in Africa, and who confine themselves to pointing out the undoubtedly too numerous errors of the missionaries and shortcomings of their flocks, would do well to consider that even if the light which has been let in is but feeble and gray it has at least dispelled a worse than Stygian darkness. As soon as native African religions—practically none of which have hitherto evolved any substantial ethical basis—develop beyond the most primitive stage they tend, notably in middle and western Africa, to grow into malign creeds of unspeakable cruelty and immorality, with a bestial and revolting ritual and ceremonial. Even a poorly taught and imperfectly understood Christianity, with its underlying foundation of justice and mercy, represents an immeasurable advance on such a creed.

Where, as in Uganda, the people are intelligent and the missionaries unite disinterestedness and zeal with common-sense, the result is astounding. The majority of the people of Uganda are now Christian, Protestant or Catholic; and many thousands among them are sincerely Christian and show their Christianity in practical fashion by putting conduct above ceremonial and dogma. Most fortunately, Protestant and Catholic seem now to be growing to work in charity together, and to show rivalry only in healthy effort against the common foe; there is certainly enough evil in the world to offer a target at which all good men can direct their shafts, without expending them on one another.

We visited the Church of England Mission, where we were received by Bishop Tucker, and the two Catholic Missions, where we were received by Bishops Hanlon and Streicher; we went through the churches and saw the schools with the pupils actually at work. In all the missions we were received with American and British flags and listened to the children singing the "Star-spangled Banner." The Church of England Mission has been at work for a quarter of a century; what has been accomplished by Bishop Tucker and those associated with him makes one of the most interesting chapters in all recent missionary history. I saw the high school,

Charles W. Hattersley, *Procession Escorting Roosevelt to the School House. Kampala in the Background*, December 21, 1909

where the sons of the chiefs are being trained in large numbers for their future duties, and I was especially struck by the admirable Medical Mission, and by the handsome cathedral, built by the native Christians themselves without outside assistance in either money or labor. At dinner at Mr. Knowles', Bishop Tucker gave us exceedingly interesting details of his past experiences in Uganda, and of the progress of the missionary work. He had been much amused by an American missionary who had urged him to visit America, saying that he would "find the latchstring outside the door"; to an American who knows the country districts well the expression seems so natural that I had never even realized that it was an Americanism.

At Bishop Hanlon's Mission, where I lunched with the bishop, there was a friend, Mother Paul, an American; before I left America, I had promised that I would surely see her, and look into the work which she, and the sisters associated with her, were doing. It was delightful seeing her; she not merely spoke my language but my neighborhood dialect. She informed me that she had just received a message of good-will for me in a letter from two of "the finest"—of course I felt at home when in mid-Africa, under the equator, I received in such fashion a message from two of

Paul Thompson, *The SS* Clement Hill *in Which Roosevelt Crossed Lake Victoria at Kisumu Pier*, December 20, 1909 the men who had served under me in the New York police. She had been teaching her pupils to sing some lines of the "Star-spangled Banner," in English, in my especial honor; and of course, had been obliged, in writing it out, to use spelling far more purely phonetic than I had ever dreamed of using. The first lines ran as follows: (Some of our word sounds have no equivalent in Uganda.)

O se ka nyu si bai di mo nseli laiti

(O say can you see by the morn's early light)

Wati so pulauli wi eli adi twayi laiti silasi giremi

(What so proudly we hailed at the twilight's last gleaming.)

After having taught the children the first verse in this manner Mother Paul said that she stopped to avoid brain fever.

In addition to scholastic exercises Mother Paul and her associates were training their school children in all kinds of industrial work, taking especial pains to develop those industries that were natural to them and would be of use when they returned to their own homes. Both at Bishop Hanlon's Mission, and at Bishop Streicher's, the Mission of the White Fathers—originally a French organization, which has established churches and schools in almost all parts of Africa—the fathers were teaching the native men to cultivate coffee, and various fruits and vegetables.

I called on the little king, who is being well trained by his English tutor—few tutors perform more exacting or responsible duties—and whose comfortable house was furnished in English fashion. I met his native advisers, shrewd, powerful-looking men; and went into the Council Chamber, where I was greeted by the council, substantial looking men, well dressed in the native fashion, and representing all the districts of the kingdom. When we visited the king, it was after dark, and we were received by smart-looking black soldiers in ordinary khaki uniform, while accompanying them were other attendants dressed in the old-time native fashion; men with flaming torches, and others with the big Uganda drums which they beat to an accompaniment of wild cries. These drums are characteristic of Uganda; each chief has one and beats upon it his own peculiar tattoo. The king, and all other people of consequence, white, Indian, or native, went round in rickshaws, one man pulling in the shafts and three others pushing behind. The rickshaw men ran well, and sang all the time, the man in the shafts serving as shanty-man, while the three behind repeated in chorus every second or two a kind of clanging note; and this went on without a break, hour after hour. The natives looked well and were dressed well; the men in long flowing garments of white, the women usually in brown cloth made in the old native style out of the bark of the bark cloth tree. The clothes of the chiefs were tastefully ornamented. All the people, gentle and simple, were very polite and ceremonious both to one another and to strangers. Now and then we met parties of Sikh soldiers, tall, bearded, fine-looking men with turbans; and there were Indian and Swahili and even Arab and Persian traders.

Charles W. Hattersley, *Roosevelt Presents Kermit to King Daudi of Uganda*, December 21, 1909

Unidentified photographer, *Roosevelt Is Standing between the Sister of Rev. W. F. Bumsted, at That Time Mother Superior of the Convent, and the Young King Daudi Chwa, and Is Surrounded by Members of the King's Court. Taken at St. Mary's Convent near Kampala*, December 21, 1909

The houses had mud walls and thatched roofs. The gardens were surrounded by braided cane fences. In the gardens and along the streets were many trees; among them bark cloth trees, from which the bark is stripped every year for cloth; great incense-trees, the sweet-scented gum oozing through wounds in the bark; and date-palms, in the fronds of which hung the nests of the golden weaverbirds, now breeding. White cow-herons, tamer than barn-yard fowls, accompanied the cattle, perching on their backs, or walking beside them. Beautiful Kavirondo cranes came familiarly round the houses. It was all strange and attractive. Birds sang everywhere. The air was heavy with the fragrance of flowers of many colors; the whole place was a riot of lush growing plants.

Through Uganda to the White Nile

As the new year dawned, the Roosevelts were already underway from Kampala northwest toward Lake Albert, the second of the two large lakes in Uganda, the other being Lake Victoria. Their larger destination was the Nile River. Upon arriving at Lake Albert, they traveled by boat for the remainder of their journey, a welcome change after months in the saddle. Slowly the expedition was making progress toward Khartoum, where it was to disband in March.

Though visits to villages, meetings with dignitaries, and hunting excursions continued, Roosevelt was drawn increasingly into political affairs back in Washington. Letters and telegrams kept him up to date with current events, and while he championed Taft's presidential campaign, he was disappointed at times with his successor's decisions. On January 7 Taft fired Roosevelt's friend Gifford Pinchot, the founding head of the United States Forest Service, a federal agency that Roosevelt had created during his administration. Upon learning the news in mid-January, Roosevelt wrote Pinchot: "I cannot believe it. I do not know any man in public life who has rendered quite the service you have rendered; and it seems to me absolutely impossible that there can be any truth in this statement." This news and other stories about the Taft administration occupied part of his mind throughout the rest of the trip. Nevertheless, the rich wildlife and scenery in the Nile Valley kept Roosevelt's spirits high.

26 January 1 to February 27, 1910

We had come down through the second of the great Nyanza lakes. As we sailed northward, its waters stretched behind us beyond the ken of vision, to where they were fed by streams from the Mountains of the Moon. On our left hand rose the frowning ranges on the other side of which the Congo forest lies like a shroud over the land. On our right we passed the mouth of the Victorian Nile, alive with monstrous crocodiles, and its banks barren of human life because of the swarms of the fly whose bite brings the torment which ends in death. As night fell, we entered the White Nile, and steamed and drifted down the mighty stream. Its current swirled in long curves between endless ranks of plumed papyrus. White and blue and red, the floating waterlilies covered the lagoons and the still inlets among the reeds; and here and there the lotus lifted its leaves and flowers stiffly above the surface. The brilliant tropic stars made lanes of light on the lapping water as we ran on through the night. The river horses roared from the reed-beds, and snorted and plunged beside the boat, and crocodiles slipped sullenly into the river as we glided by. Toward morning a mist arose and through it the crescent of the dying moon shone red and lurid. Then the sun flamed aloft and soon the African landscape, vast, lonely, mysterious, stretched on every side in a shimmering glare of heat and light; and ahead of us the great, strange river went twisting away into the distance.

At midnight we had stopped at the station of Koba, where we were warmly received by the district commissioner, and where we met half a dozen of the professional elephant hunters, who for the most part make their money, at hazard of their lives, by poaching ivory in the Congo. They are a hard-bit set, these elephant poachers; there are few careers more adventurous, or fraught with more peril, or which make heavier demands upon the daring, the endurance, and the physical hardihood of those who follow them. Elephant hunters face death at every turn, from fever, from the assaults of warlike native tribes, from their conflicts with their giant quarry; and the unending strain on their health and strength is tremendous.

At noon the following day we stopped at the deserted station of Wadelai, still in British territory. There have been outposts of white mastery on the Upper Nile for many years, but some of them are now abandoned, for as yet there has been no successful attempt at such development of the region as would alone mean permanency of occupation. The natives whom we saw offered a sharp contrast to those of Uganda; we were again back among wild savages. Near the landing at Wadelai was a group of thatched huts surrounded by a fence; there were small fields of mealies and beans, cultivated by the women, and a few cattle and goats; while big wickerwork fish-traps showed that the river also offered a means of livelihood. Both men and women were practically naked; some of the women entirely so except for a few beads. Here we were joined by an elephant hunter, Quentin Grogan, who was to show us the haunts of the great square mouthed rhinoceros, the so-called white rhinoceros, of the Lado, the only kind of African heavy game which we had not yet obtained. We were allowed to hunt in the Lado, owing to the considerate courtesy of the Belgian Government, for which I was sincerely grateful.

After leaving Wadelai we again went downstream. The river flowed through immense beds of papyrus. Beyond these on either side were rolling plains gradually rising in the distance into hills or low mountains. The plains were covered with high grass, dry and withered; and the smoke here and -there showed that the natives, according to their custom, were now burning it. There was no forest; but scattered over the plains were trees, generally thorns, but other kinds also, among them palms and euphorbias.

The following morning, forty-eight hours after leaving Butiaba, on Lake Albert Nyanza, we disembarked from the little flotilla which had carried us—a crazy little steam launch, two

J. Alden Loring, *Theodore Roosevelt at the Head of a Safari Party of African Men*, January 1910

sail-boats, and two big rowboats. We made our camp close to the river's edge, on the Lado side, in a thin grove of scattered thorn trees. The grass grew rank and tall all about us. Our tents were pitched, and the grass huts of the porters built, on a kind of promontory, the main stream running past one side, while on the other was a bay. The nights were hot and the days burning; the mosquitoes came with darkness, sometimes necessitating our putting on head nets and gloves in the evenings, and they would have made sleep impossible if we had not had mosquito biers. Nevertheless, it was a very pleasant camp, and we thoroughly enjoyed it. It was a wild, lonely country, and we saw no human beings except an occasional party of naked savages armed with bows and poisoned arrows. Game was plentiful, and a hunter always enjoys a permanent camp in a good game country; for while the expedition is marching, his movements must largely be regulated by those of the safari, whereas at a permanent camp he is foot loose.

There was an abundance of animal life, big and little, about our camp. In the reeds, and among the waterlilies of the bay, there were crocodiles, monitor lizards six feet long, and many water birds—herons, flocks of beautiful white egrets, clamorous spur-winged plover, sacred ibis, noisy purple ibis, saddle-billed storks, and lily trotters which ran lightly over the lily

Next page: Unidentified photographer, *Wadelai*, January 1910

pads. There were cormorants and snake birds. Fish eagles screamed as they circled around; very handsome birds, the head, neck, tail, breast, and forepart of the back white, the rest of the plumage black and rich chestnut. There was a queer little eagle owl with inflamed red eyelids. The black and red bulbuls sang noisily. There were many kingfishers, some no larger than chippy sparrows, and many of them brilliantly colored; some had, and others had not, the regular kingfisher voice; and while some dwelt by the riverbank and caught fish, others did not come near the water and lived on insects. There were paradise flycatchers with long, wavy white tails, and olive-green pigeons with yellow bellies. Red-headed, red-tailed lizards ran swiftly up and down the trees. The most extraordinary birds were the nightjars; the cocks carried in each wing one very long, waving plume, the pliable quill being twice the length of the bird's body and tail, and bare except for a patch of dark feather webbing at the end. The two big, dark plume tips were very conspicuous, trailing behind the bird as it flew, and so riveting the observer's attention as to make the bird itself almost escape notice. When seen flying, the first impression conveyed was of two large, dark moths or butterflies fluttering rapidly through the air; it was with a positive effort of the eye that I fixed the actual bird. The big slate and yellow bats were more interesting still. There were several kinds of bats at this camp; a small dark kind that appeared only when night had fallen and flew very near the ground all night long, and a somewhat larger one, lighter beneath, which appeared late in the evening and flew higher in the air. Both of these had the ordinary bat habits of continuous, swallow-like flight. But the habits of the slate and yellow bats were utterly different. They were very abundant, hanging in the thinly leaved acacias around the tents, and, as everywhere else, were crepuscular, indeed to a large extent actually diurnal, in habit. They saw well and flew well by daylight, passing the time hanging from twigs. They became active before sunset. In catching insects, they behaved not like swallows but like flycatchers. Except that they perched upside down so to speak, that is, that they hung from the twigs instead of sitting on them, their conduct was precisely that of a phoebe bird or a wood peewee. Each bat hung from its twig until it espied a passing insect, when it swooped down upon it, and after a short flight returned with its booty to the same perch or went on to a new one close by; and it kept twitching its long ears as it hung head downward devouring its prey.

Unidentified photographer, *Fish Trap, Wadelia*, January 1910

Next page: Unidentified photographer, *Swimming at Butiaba, Lake Albert*, January 1910

Kermit Roosevelt, *The Launch* Kenia *at Butiaba on the Shores of Lake Albert*, January 1910

White Rhinoceros

Collecting goals determined the shape of the safari's route. Indeed, the opportunity to hunt for white, or square-lipped, rhinoceros—far rarer than the black rhino, and the largest of all the living rhino species, its name coming not from the color but instead from the German *weit*, or wide—was one of the principal reasons that the expedition headed toward the Nile in the new year. Flowing northward from Lake Albert, the Nile passed through the so-called Lado Enclave, an area then part of the Belgian Congo, and now divided between South Sudan and Uganda, that was home to a population of white rhinoceros. Before the expedition's departure Belgian government officials had granted Roosevelt permission to hunt there. Although British authorities were willing to make an exception to allow him to hunt white rhinoceros on the newly established reserves—despite their recent ban of the practice—Roosevelt chose to avoid a likely public relations controversy and decided instead to save this aspect of the safari until after he had left British East Africa. There and later at Nimule and Gondokoro in Sudan, the Roosevelts pursued this celebrated animal. In addition to success with his gun, Kermit also documented the white rhinoceros with his camera.

27 February 1910

The morning after making camp we started on a rhinoceros hunt. At this time in this neighborhood, the rhinoceros seemed to spend the heat of the day in sleep, and to feed in the morning and evening, and perhaps throughout the night; and to drink in the evening and morning, usually at some bay or inlet of the river. In the morning, they walked away from the water for an hour or two, until they came to a place which suited them for the day's sleep. Unlike the ordinary rhinoceros, the square-mouthed rhinoceros feeds exclusively on grass. Its dung is very different; we only occasionally saw it deposited in heaps, according to the custom of its more common cousin. The big, sluggish beast seems fond of nosing the anthills of red earth, both with its horn and with its square muzzle; it may be that it licks them for some saline substance. It is apparently of less solitary nature than the prehensile-lipped rhino, frequently going in parties of four or five or half a dozen individuals.

We did not get an early start. Hour after hour we plodded on, under the burning sun, through the tall, tangled grass, which was often higher than our heads. Continually we crossed the trails of elephant and more rarely of rhinoceros, but the hard, sun-baked earth and stiff,

Unidentified photographer, *Native Chief Keriba Leads His Band that Escorted Roosevelt into Gondokoro*, February 1910

tinder-dry long grass made it a matter of extreme difficulty to tell if a trail was fresh, or to follow it. Finally, Kermit and his gun-bearer, Kassitura, discovered some unquestionably fresh footprints which those of us who were in front had passed over. Immediately we took the trail, Kongoni and Kassitura acting as trackers, while Kermit and I followed at their heels. Once or twice the two trackers were puzzled, but they were never entirely at fault; and after half an hour Kassitura suddenly pointed toward a thorn-tree about sixty yards off. Mounting a low anthill, I saw rather dimly through the long grass a big gray bulk, near the foot of the tree; it was a rhinoceros lying asleep on its side, looking like an enormous pig. It heard something and raised itself on its forelegs, in a sitting posture, the big ears thrown forward. I fired for the

Kermit Roosevelt, *The Great Square-Nosed Rhino of the Lado*, February 1910

214

Unidentified photographer, *The White Rhino Skins Coming into Gondokoro*, February 1910

chest, and the heavy Holland bullet knocked it clean off its feet. Squealing loudly, it rose again, but it was clearly done for, and it never got ten yards from where it had been lying.

At the shot four other rhino rose. One bolted to the right, two others ran to the left. Firing through the grass Kermit wounded a bull and followed it for a long distance, but could not overtake it; ten days later, however, he found the carcass and saved the skull and horns. Meanwhile I killed a calf, which was needed for the museum; the rhino I had already shot was a full-grown cow, doubtless the calf's mother. As the rhino rose I was struck by their likeness to the picture of the white rhino in Cornwallis Harris's folio of the big game of South Africa seventy years ago. They were totally different in look from the common rhino, seeming to stand higher and to be shorter in proportion to their height, while the hump and the huge, ungainly, square-mouthed head added to the dissimilarity. The common rhino is in color a very dark slate gray; these were a rather lighter slate gray; but this was probably a mere individual peculiarity, for the best observers say that they are of the same hue. The muzzle is broad and square, and the upper lip without a vestige of the curved, prehensile development which makes the upper lip of a common rhino look like the hook of a turtle's beak. The stomachs contained nothing but grass; it is a grazing, not a browsing animal.

There were some white egrets—not, as is usually the case with both rhinos and elephants, the cow-heron, but the slender, black-legged, yellow-toed egret—on the rhinos, and the bodies and heads of both the cow and calf looked as though they had been splashed with streaks of whitewash. One of the egrets returned after the shooting and perched on the dead body of the calf.

The heat was intense, and our gun-bearers at once began skinning the animals, lest they should spoil; and that afternoon Cuninghame and Heller came out from camp with tents, food, and water, and Heller cared for the skins on the spot, taking thirty-six hours for the job.

A Reunion in Khartoum

The final two weeks of the expedition featured little hunting and few extended stops. Aboard the steamer *Dal*, a boat supplied by Sir Reginald Wingate, the governor general of Sudan, they traveled down the Nile toward Khartoum, where Roosevelt's wife, Edith, and daughter Ethel awaited them. Roosevelt had complained about fatigue and homesickness earlier in the trip, though his letters now spoke with excitement about the safari coming to an end. To his sister Corrine, he wrote in January: "Personally I don't care if I do not fire my rifle again . . . I have enjoyed the trip to the full, and feel that it was well worth making; but I am naturally overjoyed that I am to see Edie . . . I shall never go away from her again if I can help it."

The Roosevelts reached Khartoum late in the afternoon on March 14. There they bade farewell to the Smithsonian naturalists and other members of the party. Edith and Ethel were there to welcome them. There were many stories to exchange, including the news that Roosevelt's oldest son, Ted, had recently become engaged. Wingate was also there and escorted them to the governor's palace, where they spent the night. "Long, long day," Edith wrote in her diary. "Arrived in pm. Found T and Kermit in splendid condition. Invited to stay at Palace."

28   ## February 28 to March 14, 1910

We had now finished our hunting, save that once or twice we landed to shoot a buck or some birds for the table. It was amusing to see how sharply the birds discriminated between the birds of prey which they feared and those which they regarded as harmless. We saw a flock of guinea-fowl strolling unconcernedly about at the foot of a tree in which a fish eagle was perched; and one evening Dr. Mearns saw some guinea-fowl go to roost in a bush in which two kites had already settled themselves for the night, the kites and the guineas perching amiably side by side.

We stopped at the mouth of the Sobat to visit the American Mission and were most warmly and hospitably received by the missionaries and were genuinely impressed by the faithful work they are doing, under such great difficulties and with such cheerfulness and courage. The Medical Mission was especially interesting. It formed an important part of the mission work; and not only were the natives round about treated, but those from far away also came in numbers. At the time of our visit there were about thirty patients, taking courses of treatment, who had come from distances varying from twenty-five miles to a hundred and fifty.

We steamed steadily down the Nile. Where the great river bent to the east we would sit in the shade on the forward deck during the late afternoon and look down the long glistening water-street in front of us, with its fringe of reedbed and marshy grassland and papyrus swamp, and the slightly higher dry land on which grew acacias and scattered palms. Along the riverbanks and inland were villages of Shilluks and other tribes, mostly cattle-owners; some showing slight traces of improvement, others utter savages, tall, naked men, bearing bows and arrows.

Our Egyptian and Nubian crew recalled to my mind the crew of the dahabiah [an Egyptian passenger boat] on which as a boy I had gone up the Egyptian Nile thirty-seven years before; especially when some piece of work was being done by the crew as they chanted in grunting chorus "Ya allah, ul allah." As we went down the Nile, we kept seeing more and more of the birds which I remembered, one species after another appearing: familiar cow herons, crocodile plover, noisy spur-wing plover, black and white kingfishers, hoopoos, green bee-eaters, black and white chats, desert larks, and trumpeter bullfinches.

At night we sat on deck and watched the stars and the dark, lonely river. The swimming crocodiles and plunging hippos made whirls and wakes of feeble light that glimmered for a moment against the black water. The unseen birds of the marsh and the night called to one another in strange voices. Often there were grassfires, burning, leaping lines of red, the lurid glare in the sky above them making even more sombre the surrounding gloom.

As we steamed northward down the long stretch of the Nile which ends at Khartoum, the wind blew in our faces, day after day, hard and steadily. Narrow reedbeds bordered the shore; there were grass flats and groves of acacias and palms, and farther down reaches of sandy desert. The health of our companions who had been suffering from fever and dysentery gradually improved; but the case of champagne, which we had first opened at Gondokoro, was of real service, for two members of the party were at times so sick that their situation was critical.

We reached Khartoum on the afternoon of March 14th, 1910, and Kermit and I parted from our comrades of the trip with real regret; during the year we spent together there had not been a jar, and my respect and liking for them had grown steadily. Moreover, it was a sad parting from our faithful black followers, whom we knew we should never see again. It had been an interesting and a happy year; though I was very glad to be once more with those who were dear to me, and to turn my face toward my own home and my own people.

Next page: Unidentified photographer, *The Dal Taking Wood at Bor Wood Station*, March 1910

Unidentified photographer, *Reunion at Khartoum*, March 1910

Right: Unidentified photographer, *Palace at Khartoum*, March 1910

Epilogue

Roosevelt's final chapter in *African Game Trails* ends with his party's arrival in Khartoum on March 14. He and Kermit were still more than six thousand miles from home, so their journey was far from over. Although the former president was eager to return to the familiar comforts of Sagamore Hill, it would be more than three months before he was back on Long Island. Before the trip he had expressed a desire to avoid appointments with foreign leaders en route back to the United States. His hope was to visit the Egyptian pyramids and a few favorite European destinations with his wife, Edith. Somewhat reluctantly, he agreed to deliver several speeches as well.

Roosevelt experienced a taste of what was to unfold as he steamed north to Khartoum. Three days and more than four hundred miles before he arrived at the Sudanese capital, the first boats rented by journalists and curiosity seekers met him and his party. Among others, John Callan O'Laughlin, a former assistant secretary of state in Roosevelt's administration, was there to cover his return home as a special correspondent for the *New York Times*. From there on the press was never far as he made his way out of Africa, through Europe, and back to New York. New invitations poured in to visit different countries and individuals. While he professed no interest, he found himself agreeing to more than he had initially planned.

After almost a year largely out of sight of the press, Roosevelt was once again immersing himself in both American and foreign politics. In Cairo he delivered a speech titled "Law and Order in Egypt" that commended British settlement and political engagement there. While many in London praised the speech, it drew sharp criticism from Egyptian nationalists, who spoke out against European colonialism and accused him of meddling where he did not belong. Crossing the Mediterranean and entering Italy, he again became mired in an international incident when an anticipated visit with Pope Pius X fell apart after Roosevelt refused to accept preconditions articulated by the Vatican. Pius had sought assurances that he would not meet with Methodist missionaries in Rome. Although Roosevelt did not intend to visit this group, he turned down Pius's invitation, stating publicly that he did not wish to establish a precedent whereby the

Vatican might limit the actions of the US president. Over the next couple of months, newspaper editorials kept this aborted meeting and its ramifications at the center of attention.

Much interest surrounded the question of Roosevelt's political future. He had made no public comments about his successor, but rumors—at first unsubstantiated and later found to be true—circulated about his disappointment with Taft. Two months earlier, while hunting near Lake Albert in Uganda, he received word about the removal of Gifford Pinchot as chief of the US Forest Service. He was incensed and wrote to his former associate immediately to commiserate. Now, in Italy, Roosevelt learned that Pinchot had traveled to visit with him ahead of his return to the United States. Again, the press closely followed Pinchot's journey and the eventual meeting in Porta Maurizio. On the same day as this meeting, Roosevelt wrote his friend Henry Cabot Lodge, a onetime US Representative, to express his frustration with Taft. Though the former president promised to "keep absolutely still about home politics," he expressed disbelief that Taft—whom he believed had been elected on the strength "that he would carry out my work unbroken"—had veered in new directions.

Few details about Roosevelt's intentions regarding the future emerged into public light. Nevertheless, newspapers speculated about his plans, including a run for New York governor that fall and possibly for the White House in 1912. A succession of high-profile speeches in France, Sweden, Germany, and England, as well as attendance at the funeral of British King Edward VII, followed in short order after his time in Italy, signaling his increasing attraction to the limelight. Speaking on "Citizenship in a Republic" at the Sorbonne in Paris, Roosevelt exclaimed in words befitting a once and future political candidate:

> It is not the critic who counts . . . not the man who points out how the strong man stumbles, or where the doer of deeds could have done better. The credit belongs to the man who is actually in the arena, whose face is marred by dust and sweat and blood; who strives valiantly; who errs, and comes short again and again, because there is no effort without error or shortcoming; but who does actually strive to do the deeds; who knows the great enthusiasms, the great devotions; who spends himself in a worthy cause.

For one who had deliberately removed himself from American and foreign politics, this speech hinted strongly at his desire to reenter that sphere.

Two days prior to boarding the ship that would carry him across the Atlantic, Roosevelt wrote Taft. In his first letter to his former secretary of war since the presidential inauguration fifteen months earlier, he admitted, "I do not know the situation at home." Yet, he continued: "I am of course much concerned about some of the things I see and am told; but what I have felt it best to do was to say absolutely nothing—and indeed to keep my mind as open as I kept my mouth shut!" Not wanting to complicate matters, Taft decided not to attend when Roosevelt steamed into New York Harbor aboard the ocean liner *Kaiserin Auguste Victoria* on June 18. Two days later Roosevelt turned down Taft's invitation to meet at the White House, stating, "I don't think it well for an ex-President to go to the White House, or indeed to go to Washington, except when he cannot help it. Sometime I shall have to go to Washington to look over some of the skins and skulls of the animals we collected in Africa, but I thought it would be wisest to do it when all of political Washington had left." Relations never improved, and two years later the two men would vie for the presidency in a bitter three-person contest that ultimately was won by the Democratic nominee Woodrow Wilson.

Roosevelt's welcome home reception was the largest that New York City had ever witnessed in its history. It began with an unprecedented naval pageant in New York Harbor and was followed by a six-mile-long parade through Manhattan. The *New York Times* estimated that more than a million people turned out to cheer the former president. Despite intermittent rain showers, people lined the streets and watched from windows and roofs during a three-hour procession beginning at Battery Park and running north up Broadway and Fifth Avenue. At Fifty-Ninth Street, Roosevelt and his party left the parade to attend a private lunch. Only then did crowds slowly begin to disperse.

Because of a string of obligations, Roosevelt did not arrive home on Long Island for another two days. Once back at Sagamore Hill, he rarely enjoyed any quiet over the next month, given the steady stream of visitors, regular trips back into the city, a mountain of correspondence, and the marriage of his oldest son, Theodore Roosevelt Jr., to Eleanor Butler Alexander on June 29. Though inundated with invitations, he indicated he would not make any speeches for at least two months. Instead, while Kermit went off to see college friends in Massachusetts and later that summer traveled anew to England and France, his father returned to the task of completing final revisions to his written account of the trip.

In September, *African Game Trails* appeared in bookstores. A newly edited compilation of his series of articles for *Scribner's Magazine*, the book was an immediate best-seller. Given the former president's fame, it was not altogether surprising that it became one of the most popular books of the fall season. Yet the critical reviews were decidedly mixed; most praised the vivid descriptions of African wildlife, though many expressed their disappointment with the dull monotony of ceaseless hunting scenes. The remarks by the critic for the *Philadelphia Inquirer* exemplified what many came to believe about the book. Calling it "the most important book of the season" and "an entertaining tour de force and a human document of extraordinary individuality," the writer then observed: "outside of himself, Kermit, and a few heads of

Unidentified photographer, *Mammals Exhibit, Natural History Building, Square-Lipped Rhinoceros Group*, 1913

game, nearly all other figures in the book are shadowy, and even Africa itself does not stand out very clearly. The book is avowedly Rooseveltian. That is its greatest charm."

The Roosevelt–Smithsonian Expedition amassed the largest collection of East African natural history specimens and ethnographic objects in the United States at the time. In doing so, it helped to raise the profile of the new National Museum of Natural History and furthered its commitment to original research and public education. With the charismatic former president as its main protagonist and chief chronicler, the expedition made visible the continent of Africa, its inhabitants, and its wildlife to an extent unsurpassed in its day. Yet Roosevelt's failure to see Africa with clarity and to understand more fully the Africans with whom he crossed paths is also one of this expedition's legacies. By hunting in Africa in the immediate aftermath of his presidency, Roosevelt believed that he was leaving behind Washington and American politics. In some ways, he was, though this safari represented as well the continuation of a foreign policy and a set of attitudes—pervasive in the United States and Europe—characterized by racism, colonialism, and exploitation.

Afterword

DINO J. MARTINS

The savannahs of East Africa are among the most iconic, recognizable, and celebrated of our planet's natural habitats. There is a deep connection between the savannah and the human psyche, for we are a species that was born and evolved in the African grassland ecosystems, surrounded by many other mammals, as part of a diverse community of birds, reptiles, insects, and plants, just one scrawny species among a robust, diverse assemblage of creatures.

Explorers, writers, and scientists have long romanticized and pondered our innate connection with nature. The accomplished naturalist and scientist E. O. Wilson proposed that one of the core tenets of "biophilia"—our deep need to be with and connected to other living things and the natural world—is an artifact of our species' not-so-distant (in evolutionary terms) savannah origins. As part of the early exploration and colonial venture in East Africa, a series of expeditions was undertaken in the late 1800s and early 1900s. This period was the heyday of European exploration of Africa, and East Africa in particular attracted explorers who justified their journeys as contributing to science in terms of both natural history and geography. Earlier expeditions focused on mapping, finding, and naming what were previously "undescribed" features such as mountains, rivers, and lakes, while later expeditions included finer-scale mapping but were more involved in collecting natural history specimens and ethnographic materials.

European explorers had visited Eastern Africa since the 1500s, starting with Prince Henry the Navigator, and in the nineteenth century dozens of explorers trekked into the African hinterland, including the well-known David Livingstone, later tracked down by Henry Morton Stanley, and John Hanning Speke, the supposed "discoverer" of the source of the Nile, in competition with Sir Richard Burton. Kenya was a favored destination, and expeditions there included ones led by Samuel Teleki, Ludwig Von Hohnel, and Joseph Thomson.

The Smithsonian—Roosevelt expedition of 1909–1910 followed both in the footsteps of these explorers and in the tradition of justifying the trip as a collecting expedition to support museums and science, alongside the allure of swashbuckling adventure travel. The adventure and thrill of exploration and discovery, including of hunting exotic, dangerous animals, were woven into many stories, displays, and popular culture and were portrayed as something that was worthy of the ambition

Unidentified photographer, *Old Lioness Shot by Self*, 1909–10

of civilized gentlemen who were part of the ruling, higher, or better-off social classes. Within East Africa, these expeditions and collecting trips depended on support by and field knowledge from a wide range of individuals and communities, from traders in Zanzibar and Mombasa to guides, porters, local leaders, and those who knew what routes were best to take and how to survive in a landscape that at the time posed many challenges for travelers. Though often unacknowledged, that local knowledge and support made it possible for Western explorers to undertake these journeys, for without them their expeditions would certainly have failed. A staggering amount of local labor was required, and the logistics of these journeys benefited from many different existing relationships, hierarchies, and prior knowledge. This included valuable experience gleaned from the journeys of unacknowledged or less well known African and Arab explorers, traders, and hunters.

A few explorers acknowledged the contributions made by those who shared their journeys from East Africa, but most overlooked or barely mentioned them. In *African Game Trails*, Theodore Roosevelt did mention some of the local experts, especially those who helped him track down elephants. However, most remained nameless "native guides," a backdrop to the specimens or hunting conquests celebrated in his self-focused account of the journey. This was in fact a key part of the narrative being constructed more broadly for both colonial and American imperialism. In some of the archival material from the expedition, primarily photos taken by Kermit Roosevelt, there is detail on the many guides and local support provided to the expedition. The names of the guides were recorded by Kermit, and even some of the humor in the names given to the explorers by the guides, poking fun at them. For example, he notes that one of the collectors was called "Wanna Panya" (Bwana Panya), which translates to "Mr. Rat/Rodent," speaking to his obsession with collecting small mammal specimens.

The Smithsonian—Roosevelt Expedition was one of the first expeditions to take scientific interest in animals other than big game species, collecting specimens of birds, smaller and less "charismatic" mammals, and insects. These specimens today are an important historical data point relative to the present. They provide insights into how things have changed, or not, in terms of biodiversity and habitats. An interesting coincidence about the timing of the Roosevelt Expedition in East Africa in 1909 is that the year also saw the establishment of the East Africa Natural History Society. Several colonial naturalists based in East Africa came together to establish the society and for the first time to start collecting and preserving natural history specimens *locally*, as opposed to seeing the materials carried away to European and American museums. Society members handed their collections over to the colonial government in 1931 as part of the establishment of a natural history museum in Nairobi. Today the East Africa Natural History Society remains a dynamic nature and conservation organization, now named Nature Kenya and Nature Uganda. Both organizations have a robust membership composed mainly of local naturalists and citizens from the two countries.

The establishment of museum collections, and in particular displays of animals in lifelike, dynamic postures and mounts, was both a driver and a beneficiary of these early hunting trips. Museums were becoming an important social and cultural space, and as the colonial enterprise spread across the world, they also became a vital tool in both education and propaganda for citizens of colonial states. Natural history museums became a place where people could marvel at the fabled creatures they read about in the writings of Livingstone and others. The establishment and growth of natural history collections as part of the natural history museum were an important part of increasing awareness about different parts of the world and of different animals, even if information about them was presented in a biased or limited manner. Visits to museums sparked the public's curiosity and a desire to learn more about these landscapes and their wildlife, and natural history benefited from these early expeditions as the specimens donated to or purchased by museums fueled the public's appetite—inspiring, in a virtuous circle, still more scientific expeditions and laying the groundwork for a systematic approach to understanding nature.

I grew up in rural western Kenya, and one of the highlights of the school year was a visit to the National Museum in Nairobi. I have fond memories of visiting the museum as a child, where I was obsessed with certain animals and with the insect collection. Even as our teachers tried to hurry us along I inevitably dawdled, delighting in the rows of specimens in the glass-fronted cases. I would hide from the teacher who was trying to move us along, creeping back when her gaze moved on.

Because I had seen them flitting through the rainforest canopy in Western Kenya, one of my desires was to look as closely as possible at different birds—marveling at their feet, beaks, eyes, and feathers. I spent hours in the collections observing those details that I could not see clearly in the wild and drawing them in my sketchbook. My science teacher, who was friendlier to my dawdling, had set an exercise for us to document everything we could about a particular animal or plant. As children in rural Kenya we were lucky to be surrounded by beautiful creatures, and wildlife was everywhere we looked—including in our farms and gardens. But it was a visit to the museum that turned the many wonderful, but often fleeting, glimpses of a bird into a better and fuller understanding of its shape, colors, form, and purpose. As a young naturalist I could catch insects, especially butterflies, and look at them closely, but the museum allowed me to look at the birds I enjoyed watching but couldn't quite see clearly in the rainforests. The natural history collections let me see and connect with details in a way that nothing else could at the time. This helped train me to observe more deeply and think more clearly when I returned to my rainforest home and was blessed to find the birds again in the wild.

It is by providing this ability to see, learn, and contextualize the details of nature that natural history museum collections play such an important role. In this the collections made by this and other expeditions continue to make important contributions to our understanding of nature and the myriad details of biodiversity. One of the biggest challenges we face today is the staggering loss

Kermit Roosevelt, *Two Curious Bugs We Came on on the Way to Gondokoro*, 1909–10

of species, our fellow travelers on the planet, all across the world. In East Africa the now century-old natural history collections and observation of birds have allowed scientists and conservationists to identify, map, and protect what are known as Important Bird Areas (IBAs), and this concept is being expanded to that of Important Biodiversity Areas. Knowledge of the distribution of a particular species, which scientists call biogeography, is essential to this exercise. Natural history collections and specimens provide a crucial historical part of the story, fragments of knowledge that allow us to piece together a better picture and to understand what is changing about the creatures we care about.

In Kenya today natural history collections remain an essential part of the National Museums of Kenya, which continues to play a role in both public education and awareness as well as fundamental research into biodiversity. This research is led by local scientists in collaboration with others from around the world, including the Smithsonian Institution. Through the 1970s and 1980s the National Museums of Kenya grew significantly following Richard Leakey's appointment as director, with staff numbers increasing from sixteen to more than a thousand and with many regional museums and sites brought under more rigorous management and stewardship.

Scientific collections continue to grow in East Africa. Today they and associated research programs are being established more locally within the landscapes where the discoveries are made: the Turkana Basin Institute, founded by Leakey, currently holds important fossils including of early humans at the Turkwel and Ileret Campuses in two remote counties of northern Kenya. In this way, the circle of natural history collecting is being drawn back to the communities and landscapes where this important heritage originated.

Kermit Roosevelt, *Loring with an Elephant Shrew*, 1909–10

In 2015 a scientific expedition was organized in Kenya to retrace some of the footsteps of the Smithsonian—Roosevelt expedition of 1909–1910. The "Roosevelt Resurvey" included Kenyan scientists and naturalists co-leading the numerous fieldwork and research programs. One of the amazing discoveries was an endemic rodent species on Mount Kenya. This creature was first described from the original Roosevelt specimens, then "lost" for more than a century until scientists from the National Museums of Kenya and the Smithsonian Institution caught another individual. Two data points on this little rat, over a century apart: a lesson on how much we still need to learn about the world around us.

Over the past century the world has seen immense changes across demographics, infrastructure, and landscapes. A sobering reminder of how incredibly precious the wildlife that remains is the fact that today humans and livestock make up some 96 percent of the biomass of all living mammals, with wild mammal species comprising a mere 4 percent of the total, while in 1909 there was more wildlife biomass than people and livestock. Perhaps this is the most important legacy of the Smithsonian—Roosevelt expedition in all its biased, contrived, colonial construction: that the natural world we inherit today is poorer, yes, but still so very precious that we can and must do something about it. Theodore Roosevelt wrote of the necessity of saving nature from a destructive, rapacious mankind. Today saving nature is as much as about saving humankind.

Acknowledgments

I am grateful for the support and encouragement of many people during the research and writing of this book. Kristofer Helgen, chief scientist and director of the Australian Museum Research Institute, has provided valuable assistance. Conversations with him and fellow mammologist Lauren Helgen laid the foundation for my work here. I want also to express my appreciation to Carolyn Gleason and Jaime Schwender at Smithsonian Books and to research assistants Sarah Campbell and Maya Foo. In addition, my thanks to Lonnie Bunch, the fourteenth secretary of the Smithsonian Institution, and Dino Martins, director of Stony Brook University's Turkana Basin Institute, for their written contributions.

Research for this project took me to several archives in Washington, DC, and I am grateful for the support from the dedicated librarians and archivists at the Smithsonian Institution and the Library of Congress. It is a joy to work with the collections in their care. In addition, archival research at the American Museum of Natural History, Harvard University, and the Natural History Museum in London was invaluable. I am also grateful for my colleague Amanda Skinner at the Bowdoin College Museum of Art and for the staff at the Bowdoin College Library. A final thanks to my family: to my wife, Anne; parents, Frank and Betsy; and sisters, Alison and Grace, I appreciate greatly your encouragement and many kindnesses.

Notes

Foreword

8 "The expedition yielded the specimens": Smithsonian Institution, *Annual Report of the Board of Regents* (Washington, DC: US Government Printing Office, 1910); Meg Boeni, "Theodore Roosevelt in Kenya," Smithsonian Folklife Festival Blog, August 13, 2014, https://festival.si.edu/blog/2014/theodore-roosevelt-in-kenya#:~:.; Joan Boudreau, "Clifford Berryman and the Teddy Roosevelt African Expedition," National Museum of American History, Smithsonian Institution, August 24, 2021, https://americanhistory.si.edu/explore/stories/clifford-berryman-and-teddy-roosevelt-african-expedition#:.

8 "Roosevelt was a big-game hunter": Phil Edwards, "All 512 Animals Theodore Roosevelt and His Son Killed on Safari," *Vox*, February 3, 2016, https://www.vox.com/2015/7/29/9067587/theodore-roosevelt-safari.

8 "he dishonorably discharged a regiment": "The Brownsville Incident," Theodore Roosevelt Center, Dickinson State University, n.d., https://www.theodorerooseveltcenter.org/Learn-About-TR/TR-Encyclopedia/Race-Ethnicity-and-Gender/The-Brownsville-Incident.aspx#:~:.

8 "a notorious book that promulgated scientific racism": Jedediah Purdy, "Environmentalism's Racist History," *The New Yorker*, August 13, 2015, https://www.newyorker.com/news/news-desk/environmentalisms-racist-history.

9 "Buganda compelled Roosevelt to rethink his fundamental assumptions": Jonathon L. Earle, "The Real Wakanda: How an East African Kingdom Changed Theodore Roosevelt and the Course of American Democracy," *Politico*, March 10, 2023, https://www.politico.com/news/magazine/2023/03/10/east-african-kingdom-theodore-roosevelt-00085962.

Introduction

The story of Roosevelt's 1909–1910 expedition to East Africa has been recounted by various historians in his own day and more recently. The most comprehensive recent accounts include Bartle Bull, *Safari: A Chronicle of Adventure* (New York: Viking, 1988); Patricia O'Toole, *When Trumpets Call: Theodore Roosevelt after the White House* (New York: Simon & Schuster, 2005); J. Lee Thompson, *Theodore Roosevelt Abroad: Nature, Empire, and the Journey of an American President* (New York: Palgrave Macmillan, 2010); and Michael R. Canfield, *Theodore Roosevelt in the Field* (Chicago: University of Chicago Press, 2015).

11 "likely to do some hunting": "Roosevelt's World Tour," *Boston Globe*, April 15, 1908.

11 "the article concluded": "Roosevelt to Stay Abroad Two Years," *New York Times*, May 2, 1908.

11 "The trip, the *Times* wrote": "Roosevelt's Plans for Big Game Hunt," *New York Times*, June 6, 1908.

14 "something he longed to do": On Roosevelt's legacy as a hunter and a conservationist, see Douglas Brinkley, *The Wilderness Warrior: Theodore Roosevelt and the Crusade for America* (New York: HarperCollins, 2009); R. L. Wilson, *Theodore Roosevelt: Outdoorsman* (New York: Winchester Press, 1971); Canfield, *Theodore Roosevelt in the Field.*

14 "great admiration for men who were fearless": Theodore Roosevelt, *An Autobiography* (New York: Charles Scribner's Sons, 1913), 280.

14 "exercise its power or risk losing it": On the perceived crisis of masculinity in turn-of-the-century America, see Gail Bederman, *Manliness and Civilization: A Cultural History of Gender and Race in the United States, 1880–1917* (Chicago: University of Chicago Press, 1995).

16 "Selous was impressed": Frederick Selous, *African Nature Notes and Reminiscences* (London: Macmillan, 1908), viii.

18 "the racist perception of Africa": On America's engagement with Africa, see Jeannette Jones, *In Search of Brightest Africa: Reimagining the Dark Continent in American Culture, 1884–1936* (Athens: University of Georgia Press, 2010).

18 "I would like to get a few trophies": Theodore Roosevelt to George Otto Trevelyan, June 19, 1908, in *The Letters of Theodore Roosevelt*, ed. Elting E. Morison (Cambridge, MA: Harvard University Press), 6:1089.

19 "I had something to do with their arrangement": Carl Akeley, *In Brightest Africa* (Garden City, NY: Garden City Publishing Co., 1920), 158–59. In this volume Akeley lists their meeting date as 1906. However, in a later essay, he corrects the date. See Carl Akeley, "Roosevelt in Africa," in Theodore Roosevelt, *African Game Trails* (New York: Charles Scribner's Sons, 1924), ix–xx.

19 "settlement, trade, and tourism": On the Uganda Railway, see Charles Miller, *The Lunatic Express: An Entertainment on Imperialism* (London: Macmillan, 1971).

21 "I do not think he is a very sound sportsman": Edward Buxton to Theodore Roosevelt, April 28, 1908, Letter in the Theodore Roosevelt Papers, Library of Congress (TRP-LC), Washington, DC.

21 "I trust that I shall have as good luck as you had": Theodore Roosevelt to Whitelaw Reid, August 20, 1908, in Morison, ed., *Letters*, 6:1186; Theodore Roosevelt to Whitelaw Reid, January 6, 1909, ibid., 6:1465; and Theodore Roosevelt to Winston Churchill, January 6, 1909, ibid., 6:1467.

21 "routinely were permitted to pursue big game": Paul Munro, "Colonial Wildlife Conservation and National Parks in Sub-Saharan Africa," *African History, Oxford Research Encyclopedias*, 2021, https://oxfordre.com/africanhistory/display/10.1093/acrefore/9780190277734.001.0001/acrefore-9780190277734-e-195.

23 "the way the British authorities are treating me": Theodore Roosevelt to Whitelaw Reid, November 26, 1908, in Morison, ed., *Letters*, 6:1383, 1385.

23 "sentimentalizing and humanizing the lives of wild animals": John Burroughs, "Real and Sham Natural History," *Atlantic Monthly*, March 1903.

23 "working for the preservation and perpetuation of the wildlife": Theodore Roosevelt, *Outdoor Pastimes of an American Hunter* (New York: Charles Scribner's Sons, 1905), v–vi, 377–78.

24 "an interest that is at once scientific and thoroughly human": John Burroughs, *Camping and Tramping with Roosevelt* (Boston: Houghton Mifflin Company, 1906), 7, 79–80.

24 "he identified Long again": "Roosevelt Only a Game Killer—Long," *New York Times*, May 23, 1908; "Long Writes Roosevelt," *New York Times*, May 24, 1907; Theodore Roosevelt, "Nature Fakers," *Everybody's Magazine*, September 1907.

25 "I am no butcher": Theodore Roosevelt to John Patterson, March 20, 1908, in Morison, ed., *Letters*, 6:978–79.

25 "Roosevelt also drafted a short foreword": Theodore Roosevelt, "Extract from Message from the Hon. Theodore Roosevelt, President of the United States," *Journal of the Society for the Preservation of the Wild Fauna of the Empire* 4 (1908): 8.

28 "don't let anything divert you": Theodore Roosevelt to Kermit Roosevelt, April 23, 1908, letter in the Theodore Roosevelt Collection (TRC-H), Houghton Library, Harvard University.

28 "buckling down to hard, plodding work": Theodore Roosevelt to Kermit Roosevelt, May 17, 1908, letter, TRC-H.

28 "probably we ought each to have a spare rifle": Theodore Roosevelt to Kermit Roosevelt, June 6, 1908, letter, TRC-H.

29 "His book should be translated into English at once": Theodore Roosevelt, quoted in an advertisement for *With Flashlight and Rifle* in Carl Schillings, *In Wildest Africa* (London: Hutchinson & Co., 1907). On the subject of recording wildlife with a camera, see Gregg Mitman, *Reel Nature: America's Romance with Wildlife on Film* (Cambridge, MA: Harvard University Press, 1999); and James Ryan, *Picturing Empire: Photography and the Visualization of the British Empire* (Chicago: University of Chicago Press, 1997).

29 "camera hunting takes twice the man that gun hunting takes": Harry Johnston, quoted in Carl Schillings, *With Flashlight and Rifle* (London: Hutchinson & Co., 1905), xiv; Akeley, *In Brightest Africa*, 155.

29 "Lang was available to accompany the expedition": Frank Chapman to Theodore Roosevelt, June 5, 1908, letter, TRP-LC; Theodore Roosevelt to Frank Chapman, June 7, 1908, in Morison, ed., *Letters*, 6:1061; Frank Chapman to Theodore Roosevelt, July 3, 1908, letter, TRP-LC.

30 "we will be able to pick enough that we want": Theodore Roosevelt to Kermit Roosevelt, October 27, 1908, letter, TRC-H.

30 "not taking it with sufficient seriousness": Theodore Roosevelt to William Taft, September 11, 1908, in Morison, ed., *Letters*, 6:1231; Theodore Roosevelt to William Taft, September 5, 1908, ibid., 6:1209–10.

31 "we are immensely interested in your African project": Robert Bridges to Theodore Roosevelt, June 10, 1908, letter, TRP-LC.

31 "he would be paid $12,000 annually": Samuel McClure to Theodore Roosevelt, July 1, 1908, letter, TRP-LC; Theodore Roosevelt to Robert Bridges, July 2, 1908, letter, TRC-LC ; Theodore Roosevelt to Robert Collier, July 9, 1908, in Morison, ed., *Letters*, 6:1115.

31 "who always try to practice what they preach": Theodore Roosevelt to Henry Cabot Lodge, August 8, 1908, in Morison, ed., *Letters*, 6:1161–63.

33 "the museum to which my collection should go": Theodore Roosevelt to Charles Walcott, June 20, 1908, ibid., 6:1093.

34 "I should like to remain a man of action as long as possible": Theodore Roosevelt to Henry Cabot Lodge, June 24, 1908, ibid., 6:1096.

34 "I don't want any more trophies": Cyrus Adler to Theodore Roosevelt, June 23, 1908, letter, TRP-LC; Charles Walcott to Theodore Roosevelt, June 27, 1908, letter, TRP-LC; Theodore Roosevelt to Henry Cabot Lodge, August 8, 1908, in Morison, ed., *Letters*, 6:1162.

35 "almost every letter brought some reference to preparations": Kermit Roosevelt, *The Happy Hunting-Grounds* (New York: Charles Scribner's Sons, 1920), 16.

35 "by means of national parks and forest reserves": Theodore Roosevelt, *African Game Trails* (New York: Charles Scribner's Sons, 1910), 22–24.

36 "how delicious he had found it in the Bad Lands": Roosevelt, *The Happy Hunting Grounds*, 18.

36 "he demanded that they remove all such notices": Ezra Fitch to Theodore Roosevelt, November 21, 1908, letter, TRP-LC; and Ezra Fitch to Theodore Roosevelt, December 2, 1908, letter, TRP-LC.

36 "totally foreign to the life and the country": Roosevelt, *The Happy Hunting-Grounds*, 29.

36 "he and Loomis refined the library": John Loomis to Theodore Roosevelt, November 24, 1908, letter, TRP-LC; John Loomis to Theodore Roosevelt, February 19, 1909, letter, TRP-LC.

37 "go out among your people": "Editorial Notes," *New York Observer and Chronicle*, January 23, 1908.

37 "before you can start on your hunt": Theodore Roosevelt to Whitelaw Reid, May 25, 1908, in Morison, ed., *Letters*, 6:1036; Frederick Selous to Theodore Roosevelt, November 29, 1908, letter, TRP-LC.

39 "exactly the justification I require": Theodore Roosevelt to George N. Curzon, August 18, 1908, in Morison, ed., *Letters*, 6:1177–78.

40 "I am looking forward to the trip": Theodore Roosevelt to Cecil Arthur Spring Rice, September 17, 1908, ibid., 6:1241–42.

40 "accidents limited his physical preparations": Roosevelt, *The Happy-Hunting Grounds*, 20–21.

41 "the boy may commit some imprudence": Whitelaw Reid to Theodore Roosevelt, February 23, 1909, letter, TRP-LC.

41 "their journey through the territory would proceed uninterrupted": "The Acting Governor," *The East African Standard*, April 17, 1909.

41 "I don't wish to be falsely modest in this": William Taft to Theodore Roosevelt, November 7, 1908, letter, TRP-LC.

43 "I was their President": Theodore Roosevelt to Kermit Roosevelt, February 13, 1909, letter, TRC-H.

43 "Theodore Roosevelt always followed that maxim": Corinne Robinson, *My Brother Theodore Roosevelt* (New York: Charles Scribner's Sons, 1921), 248.

45 "enterprising apostles of sensationalism": Theodore Roosevelt to Robert Bridges, August 14, 1908, in Morison, ed., *Letters*, 6:1172.

45 "seeking the assistance of local authorities": Theodore Roosevelt to Melville Stone, December 2, 1908, ibid., 6:1403–5; Melville Stone to Theodore Roosevelt, December 4, 1908, letter, TRP-LC; and Theodore Roosevelt to Whitelaw Reid, December 4, 1908, letter in the Whitelaw Reid Collection, Library of Congress, Washington, DC.

45 "the press's desire for access": Lawrence Abbott, *Impressions of Theodore Roosevelt* (Garden City, NY: Doubleday, Page & Co., 1919), 200.

47 "he will take his place in history with Washington and Lincoln": "Roosevelt the Man, Estimated by Taft," *New York Times*, March 4, 1909.

47 "I am a private citizen": Theodore Roosevelt, "A Scientific Expedition," *The Outlook*, March 20, 1909.

African Game Trails: Twenty-Eight Excerpts

64 "not a single chair was vacant": "Arrival of Ex-President Roosevelt," *The East African Standard*, April 24, 1909.

71 "large American flag flying": "The Roosevelt-Smithsonian Expedition," *The East African Standard*, May 1, 1909.

94 "I have had no time to write": Theodore Roosevelt to Robert Bridges, May 12, 1909, letter, TRP-LC.

100 "securing more than four thousand specimens": "In Memoriam: Edgar Alexander Mearns," *The Auk: A Quarterly Journal of Ornithology*, January 1918, 14–15.

104 "he is a bold rider": Theodore Roosevelt to Theodore Roosevelt, III, May 17, 1909, in *The Letters of Theodore Roosevelt*, ed. Elting E. Morison (Cambridge, MA: Harvard University Press), 7:10.

104 "from the standpoint of science in America": Theodore Roosevelt to Andrew Carnegie, June 1, 1909, in Morison, ed., *Letters*, 7:13–15.

104 "Walcott released their names in 1913": In 1913, Smithsonian Secretary Charles Walcott publicized a list of contributors to the expedition. In addition to Carnegie, more than two dozen other individuals donated. Walcott explained that the Smithsonian underwrote 60 percent of the expedition's cost and that Roosevelt contributed the other 40 percent. "Helped to Finance Roosevelt's Hunt," *New York Times*, February 17, 1913.

111 "let the public have occasional authentic news": Francis W. Dawson, *Opportunity and Theodore Roosevelt* (New York: Honest Truth Publishing Co., 1923), 63.

111 "the same detestable business": William J. Long, "Long Attacks Roosevelt," *New York Times*, May 27, 1909. "he wanted rest from his usual preoccupations": Dawson, *Opportunity and Theodore Roosevelt*, 135.

128 "We shall have to let the papers know": Ibid., 107, 109.

135 "not of years but of many generations": Ibid., 167, 181.

135 "riding well and pluckily": Theodore Roosevelt to Ethel Roosevelt, August 1, 1909, letter, TRC-LC.

145 "the movie about East Africa": Cherry Kearton, *Photographing Wild Life across the World* (London: J. W. Arrowsmith, 1923), 105.

157 "Cook, though a capable man, is a fake": Theodore Roosevelt to Anna Roosevelt Cowles, October 17, 1909, in Morison, ed., *Letters*, 7:38.

166 "Twenty is hardier and more active": Theodore Roosevelt to Anna Cowles, October 17, 1909, letter, TRC-LC.

166 "the conditions of this new country": Dawson, *Opportunity and Theodore Roosevelt*, 155.

180 "I felt certain it would eventually meet with just appreciation": Carl Akeley, *In Brightest Africa* (Garden City, NY: Garden City Publishing Co., 1920), 161.

185 "after failing to get pictures of several lions": Ibid., 166.

196 "to do it just as well as I possibly can": Theodore Roosevelt to Ethel Roosevelt, December 12, 1909, letter, TRC-LC.

203 "it seems to me absolutely impossible": Theodore Roosevelt to Gifford Pinchot, January 17, 1910, letter in the Gifford Pinchot Papers, Library of Congress, Washington, DC.

218 "I shall never go away from her again": Theodore Roosevelt to Corrine Robinson, January 21, 1910, letter, TRC-LC.

218 "Invited to stay at Palace": Edith Roosevelt, March 14, 1910, diary, TRP-LC.

Epilogue

225 "veered in new directions": Theodore Roosevelt to Henry Cabot Lodge, April 11, 1910, in *The Letters of Theodore Roosevelt*, ed. Elting E. Morison (Cambridge, MA: Harvard University Press), 7:70–71.

225 "who spends himself in a worthy cause": Quoted in "Roosevelt Idea of Good Citizen," *New York Times*, April 24, 1910.

226 "say absolutely nothing": Theodore Roosevelt to William Taft, June 8, 1910, in Morison, ed., *Letters*, 7:88–89.

226 "when all of political Washington had left": Theodore Roosevelt to William Taft, June 20, 1910, in Morison, ed., *Letters*, 7:93.

226 "more than a million people turned out": "Million Saw the Parade," *New York Times*, June 19, 1910.

226 "he would not make any speeches for at least two months": "Roosevelt to Be Silent Two Months," *New York Times*, June 16, 1910. Of note, Roosevelt's first speech after his return was before the National Negro Business League in New York City. On that occasion, he reiterated his recommendation that African Americans dedicate themselves to work and education as opposed to political action. That summer, at the invitation of educator Booker T. Washington, Roosevelt also joined the Board of Trustees at the Tuskegee Normal and Industrial Institute, one of the nation's leading educational institutions for African Americans. Roosevelt's perspective on issues of race aligned closely with figures such as Washington, who favored education and a gradualist approach to change.

227 "That is its greatest charm": "Newest and Best in the Book World," *Philadelphia Inquirer*, September 12, 1910.

Afterword

228 "core tenets of 'biophilia'": E. O. Wilson, *Biophilia: The Human Bond with Other Species* (Cambridge, MA: Harvard University Press, 1984).

228 "justified their journeys as contributing to science": A. A. Mazrui, "European Exploration and Africa's Self-Discovery," *Journal of Modern African Studies* 7, no. 4 (1969): 661–76.

228 "mountains, rivers, and lakes": J. C. Stone, "Imperialism, Colonialism and Cartography," *Transactions of the Institute of British Geographers* 13, no. 1 (1988): 57–64.

230 "a wide range of individuals and communities": W. Beinart, K. Brown, and D. Gilfoyle, "Experts and Expertise in Colonial Africa Reconsidered: Science and the Interpenetration of Knowledge," *African Affairs* 108, no. 432 (2009): 413–33.

232 "known as Important Bird Areas": L. Bennun and P. Njoroge, "Important Bird Areas in Kenya," *Ostrich* 71, nos. 1–2 (2000): 164–67.

232 "provide a crucial historical part of the story": A. M. Lister, "Natural History Collections as Sources of Long-Term Datasets," *Trends in Ecology & Evolution* 26, no. 4 (2011): 153–54.

233 "comprising a mere 4 percent of the total": Y. M. Bar-On, R. Phillips, and R. Milo, "The Biomass Distribution on Earth," *Proceedings of the National Academy of Sciences* 115, no. 25 (2018): 6506–11.

Selected Bibliography

Abbott, Lawrence. *Impressions of Theodore Roosevelt*. Garden City, NY: Doubleday, Page & Co., 1919.

Abbott, Lawrence, ed. *The Letters of Archie Butt, Personal Aide to President Roosevelt*. Garden City, NY: Doubleday, Page, and Co., 1924.

Akeley, Carl. *In Brightest Africa*. Garden City, NY: Garden City Publishing Co., 1920.

Aldrick, Judy. *Northrup: The Life of William Northrup McMillan*. Kijabe, Kenya: Old Africa Books, 2012.

Ambler, Charles. *Kenyan Communities in the Age of Imperialism*. New Haven, CT: Yale University Press, 1988.

Bederman, Gail. *Manliness and Civilization: A Cultural History of Gender and Race in the United States, 1880–1917*. Chicago: University of Chicago Press, 1995.

Brinkley, Douglas. *The Wilderness Warrior: Theodore Roosevelt and the Crusade for America*. New York: HarperCollins, 2009.

Brooks, Sydney. "What Europe Thinks of Roosevelt." *McClure's Magazine*, July 1910.

Bull, Bartle. *Safari: A Chronicle of Adventure*. New York: Viking, 1988.

Burroughs, John. *Camping and Tramping with Roosevelt*. Boston: Houghton Mifflin Company, 1906.

———. "Theodore Roosevelt." *Natural History*, January 1919.

Butt, Archibald. *Taft and Roosevelt: The Intimate Letters of Archie Butt, Military Aide*. Garden City, NY: Doubleday, Doran & Co., 1930.

Buxton, Edward. *Two African Trips*. London: Edward Stanford, 1902.

Cameron, Kenneth. *Into Africa: The Story of the East Africa Safari*. London: Constable, 1990.

Canfield, Michael R. *Theodore Roosevelt in the Field*. Chicago: University of Chicago Press, 2015.

Cannadine, David. *Ornamentalism: How the British Saw Their Empire*. Oxford: Oxford University Press, 2001.

Chapman, Abel. *On Safari: Big Game Hunting in British East Africa*. London: Edward Arnold, 1908.

Churchill, Winston. *My African Journey*. London: Hodder and Stoughton, 1908.

Cotton, Edward. *The Ideals of Theodore Roosevelt*. New York: D. Appleton and Company, 1923.

Cowles, Anna Roosevelt. *Letters from Theodore Roosevelt to Anna Roosevelt Cowles, 1870–1918*. New York: Charles Scribner's Sons, 1924.

Cranworth, Lord. *A Colony in the Making, or Sport and Profit in British East Africa*. London: Macmillan, 1912.

———. "Game Preservation in East Africa." *National Review*, May 1907.

Cutwright, Paul. *Theodore Roosevelt: The Making of a Conservationist*. Urbana: University of Illinois Press, 1985.

Dawson, Francis. "Hunting with Roosevelt in East Africa." *Hampton's Magazine*, November 1909.

———. *Opportunity and Theodore Roosevelt*. New York: Honest Truth Publishing Co., 1923.

Dugmore, A. Radclyffe. *Camera Adventures in the African Wilds*. New York: Doubleday, Page, and Co. 1910.

Everett, Marshall. *Roosevelt's Thrilling Experiences in the Wilds of Africa Hunting Big Game*. New York: J. T. Moss, 1909.

Foran, W. Robert. *With Roosevelt in Africa*. London: Robert Hale, 1924.

Gerstle, Gary. "Theodore Roosevelt and the Divided Character of American Nationalism." *Journal of American History* 86, no. 3 (December 1999): 1280–1307.

Goodwin, Doris Kearns. *The Bully Pulpit: Theodore Roosevelt, William Howard Taft, and the Golden Age of Journalism*. New York: Simon & Schuster, 2013.

Haraway, Donna. *Primate Visions*. New York: Routledge, 1989.

Herman, Daniel. *Hunting and the American Imagination*. Washington, DC: Smithsonian Institution Press, 2001.

Hoyt, Edwin. *Teddy Roosevelt in Africa*. New York: Duell, Sloan and Pearce, 1966.

Huxley, Elspeth. *White Man's Country: Lord Delamere and the Making of Kenya*. New York: Praeger, 1967.

Irwin, Will, ed. *Letters to Kermit from Theodore Roosevelt, 1902–1908*. New York: Charles Scribner's Sons, 1946.

Johnston, Alex. *The Life and Letters of Sir Harry Johnston*. London: Jonathan Cape, 1929.

Johnston, Harry. "The Roosevelts in Africa." *The Outlook*, December 17, 1910.

———. *The Story of My Life*. Indianapolis: Bobs-Merrill Company, 1923.

Jones, Jeannette. *In Search of Brightest Africa: Reimagining the Dark Continent in American Culture, 1884–1936*. Athens: University of Georgia Press, 2010.

Kearton, Cherry. *Photographing Wildlife across the World*. London: J. W. Arrowsmith, 1923.

Kennedy, David. *Islands of White: Settler Society and Culture in Kenya and Southern Rhodesia, 1890–1939*. Durham, NC: Duke University Press, 1987.

Lodge, Henry Cabot, ed. *Selections from the Correspondence of Theodore Roosevelt and Henry Cabot Lodge, 1884–1918*. New York: Charles Scribner's Sons, 1925.

Loring, J. Alden. *African Adventure Stories*. New York: Charles Scribner's Sons, 1914.

Mackenzie, John. *The Empire of Nature: Hunting, Conservation and British Imperialism*. Manchester: Manchester University Press, 1988.

Madeira, Percy. *Hunting in British East Africa*. London: J. B. Lippincott, 1909.

Maxon, Robert. *John Ainsworth and the Making of Kenya*. Lanham, MD: University Press of America, 1980.

McLynn, Frank. *Hearts of Darkness: The European Exploration of Africa*. New York: Carroll & Graf, 1992.

Miller, Charles. *Gifford Pinchot and the Making of Modern Environmentalism*. Washington, DC: Island Press, 2001.

———. *The Lunatic Express: An Entertainment on Imperialism*. London: Macmillan, 1971.

Mitman, Gregg. *Reel Nature: America's Romance with Wildlife on Film*. Cambridge, MA: Harvard University Press, 1999.

Morison, Elting, ed. *The Letters of Theodore Roosevelt*. Cambridge, MA: Harvard University Press, 1952.

Morris, Charles. *Battling for the Right: The Life-Story of Theodore Roosevelt*. Philadelphia: W. E. Scull, 1910.

Morris, Edmund. *Theodore Rex*. New York: Random House, 2001.

Morris, Sylvia. *Edith Kermit Roosevelt: Portrait of a First Lady*. New York: Vintage Books, 1990.

Mowbray, John. *Roosevelt's Marvelous Exploits in the Wilds of Africa*. New York: George W. Bertron, 1909.

O'Laughlin, John Callan. *From the Jungle through Europe with Roosevelt*. Boston: Chapple, 1910.

Oliver, Roland. *Sir Harry Johnston and the Scramble for Africa*. London: Chatto & Windus, 1964.

Osborn, Henry Fairfield. *Impressions of Great Naturalists*. New York: Charles Scribner's Sons, 1924.

O'Toole, Patricia. *When Trumpets Call: Theodore Roosevelt after the White House*. New York: Simon & Schuster, 2005.

Patterson, John. *The Man-Eaters of Tsavo, and Other East African Adventures*. London: Macmillan and Co., 1907.

Pavitt, Nigel. *Kenya: A Country in the Making, 1880–1940*. New York: W. W. Norton, 2008.

Peary, Robert. *The North Pole*. London: John Murray, 1910.

Pinchot, Gifford. *Breaking New Ground*. New York: Harcourt Brace, 1947.

Pratt, Mary L. *Imperial Eyes*. London: Routledge, 1992

Robinson, Corinne. *My Brother Theodore Roosevelt*. New York: Charles Scribner's Sons, 1921.

Roosevelt, Kermit. *The Happy Hunting-Grounds*. New York: Charles Scribner's Sons, 1920.

Roosevelt, Theodore. *African and European Addresses*. New York: Charles Scribner's Sons, 1910.

———. *African Game Trails*. New York: Charles Scribner's Sons, 1910.

———. *An Autobiography*. New York: Charles Scribner's Sons, 1913.

———. *Outdoor Pastimes of an American Hunter*. New York: Charles Scribner's Sons, 1905.

———. *The Strenuous Life: Essays and Addresses*. New York: Century, 1901.

Ryan, James. *Picturing Empire: Photography and the Visualization of the British Empire*. Chicago: University of Chicago Press, 1997.

Schillings, Carl. *In Wildest Africa*. London: Hutchinson and Co., 1907.

———. *With Flashlight and Rifle*. London: Hutchinson and Co., 1905.

Selous, Frederick Courtenay. *African Nature Notes and Reminiscences*. London: Macmillan, 1908.

Seymour, Frederick. *Roosevelt in Africa*. New York: D. B. McCurdy, 1909.

Steinhart, Edward. *Black Poachers, White Hunters: A Social History of Hunting in Colonial Kenya*. Athens: Ohio University Press, 2006.

Stewart, Kate. "Theodore Roosevelt: Hunter-Naturalist on Safari." *Quarterly Journal of the Library of Congress*, July 1970, 242–56.

Taylor, Stephen. *The Mighty Nimrod: A Life of Frederick Courtenay Selous, African Hunter and Adventurer, 1851–1917*. London: Collins, 1989.

Thompson, J. Lee. *Theodore Roosevelt Abroad: Nature, Empire, and the Journey of an American President*. New York: Palgrave Macmillan, 2010.

Thomson, Joseph. *Through Masai Land*. London: Frank Cass, 1968.

Tilchin, William. *Theodore Roosevelt and the British Empire*. New York: St. Martin's Press, 1997.

Tobias, Ronald. *Film and the American Moral Vision: Theodore Roosevelt to Walt Disney*. East Lansing: Michigan State University Press, 2011.

Trzebinski, Errol. *The Kenya Pioneers*. New York: W. W. Norton, 1988.

Unger, Frederick. *Roosevelt's Hunting Trip in Africa*. Chicago: Charles Thompson, 1909.

Wallihan, Allen Grant. *Camera Shots at Big Game*. New York: Doubleday, Page and Co., 1901.

Warburg, Gabriel. *The Sudan under Wingate*. London: Frank Cass and Co., 1971.

West, Nicholas. *Happy Valley: The Story of the English in Kenya*. London: Secker and Warburg, 1979.

Wilson, R. L. *Theodore Roosevelt: Outdoorsman*. New York: Winchester Press, 1971.

Wood, Frederick. *Roosevelt as We Knew Him*. Philadelphia: J. C. Winston, 1927.

Youssuf, Ali. "Egypt's Reply to Colonel Roosevelt." *North American Review*, June 1910.

Image Credits

American Museum of Natural History Library:
229: Asset ID: ppc_r65_sc_c049; **232**: Asset ID: ppc_r65_sg_g199; **233**: Asset ID: ppc_r65_sb_b115.

Library of Congress, Washington, DC, Prints and Photographs Division:
17: LC-B2-173-11 [P & P]; **22**: (STEREO PRES FILE - Roosevelt, Theodore - Western Tour - Wyoming - 1903 [item] [P & P].

Mapping Specialists Ltd.:
Endsheets; 48.

National Portrait Gallery, Smithsonian Institution:
15: Gift of Joanna Sturm, NPG.81.122; **18**: NPG.93.81; **26**: Gift of Joanna Sturm, NPG.81.126; **42**: NPG.80.198.

National Portrait Gallery—London:
20: Given by Martin Plaut, 2012, NPG P1700 (86d).

Private Collection:
50*l*, **50***r*; **61**.

Smithsonian Institution Archives:
7: Record Unit 7179, Box 4, Folder 11; **33**: Record Unit 95, Box 23, Folder 21B; **62**: Record Unit 7179, Box 3, Folder 39; **65**: Record Unit 7179, Box 4, Folder 39; **72**: Record Unit 7179, Box 4, Folder 21; **92**: Record Unit 7179, Box 5, Folder 65; **96**: Record Unit 7179, Box 4, Folder 40; **105**: Record Unit 7179, Box 3, Folder 75; **107**: Record Unit 7179, Box 3, Folder 75; **116**: Record Unit 7179, Box 2, Folder 14; **119**: Record Unit 7179, Box 4, Folder 11; **123**: Record Unit 7179, Box 3, Folder 61; **132**: Record Unit 7179, Box 2, Folder 22; **138**: Record Unit 7179, Box 4, Folder 39; **150**: Record Unit 7179, Box 4, Folder 47; **160**: Record Unit 7179, Box 3, Folder 72; **164**: Record Unit 7179, Box 3, Folder 75; **170**: Record Unit 7179, Box 4, Folder 27; **173**: Record Unit 7179, Box 4, Folder 25; **176**: Record Unit 7179, Box 4, Folder 25; **179**: Record Unit 7179, Box 2, Folder 38; **188**: Record Unit 7179, Box 4, Folder 5; **206**: Record Unit 7179, Box 3, Folder 64; **208**: Record Unit 7179, Box 3, Folder 64; **210**: Record Unit 7179, Box 3, Folder 43; **215**: Record Unit 7179, Box 3, Folder 24; **220**: Record Unit 7179, Box 4, Folder 41; **223**: Record Unit 7179, Box 4, Folder 46; **227**: Record Unit 95, Box 44A, Folder 1.

Theodore Roosevelt Collection, Houghton Library, Harvard University:

2: 560.61.R67k2-116; **9**: R560.61.R67k1-079; **12**: 560.11-021; **13**: 520.14-003; **38**: 560.52 1905-168; **44**: 560.52 1909-006; **46**: 560.52 1909-015; **53**: 560.61-170; **56**: 560.61-002; **57**: 560.61-006; **58**: 560.61-018; **60**: 560.61-031; **67**: 560.61-049; **69**: 560.61-184; **70**: 560.61.R67k2-116; **73**: 560.61-252; **74**: 560.61-191; **75**: 560.61-251; **77**: 560.61.R67k1-002; **78**: 560.61-119; **79**: 560.61.R67k2-013; **82**: 560.61-193; **84**: 560.61-263; **87**: 560.61-115; **89**: 560.61-281; **90**: 560.61-152; **95**: 560.61-173; **97**: 560.61-053; **98**: 560.61-056; **101**: 560.61-214; **102**: 560.61.R67k2-111; **103**: 560.61-146; **108**: 560.61.R67k1-003; **110**: 560.61-238; **113**: 560.61-178; **114**: 560.61-222; **117**: 560.61-164; **121**: R560.61.R67k1-074; **126**: 560.61-233; **127**: R560.61.R67k1-027; **129**: 560.61-288; **130**: R560.61.R67k2-080; **131**: 560.61-250; **136**: 560.61-058; **137**: 560.61-059; **142**: R560.61.R67k1-081; **143**: 560.61-290; **144**: 560.61.R67k1-077; **146**: R560.61.R67k1-097; **147**: R560.61.R67k1-092; **148**: 560.61.R67k1-094; **153**: R560.61.R67k2-008; **154**: R560.61.R67k2-150; **155**: R560.61.R67k2-152; **158**: R560.61.R67k2-058; **162**: R560.61.R67k2-134; **167**: 560.61-063d; **169**: R560.61.R67k2-156; **172**: R560.61.R67k1-218; **175**: 560.61-201; **182**: R560.61.R67k2-062; **183**: R560.61.R67k2-053; **184**: 560.61-111; **187**: R560.61.R67k2-075; **190**: R560.61.R67k2-070; **191**: R560.61.R67k1-140; **194**: R560.61.R67k2-036; **198**: 560.61-064; **199**: 560.61-068; **201**: 560.61-07; **202**: 560.61-079; **205**: R560.61.R67k1-079; **212**: 560.61-267; **214**: R560.61.R67k1-242; **216**: R560.61.R67k1-213; **222**: 500.R67-134.

Index

Note: Illustrations are indicated by page numbers in italics.

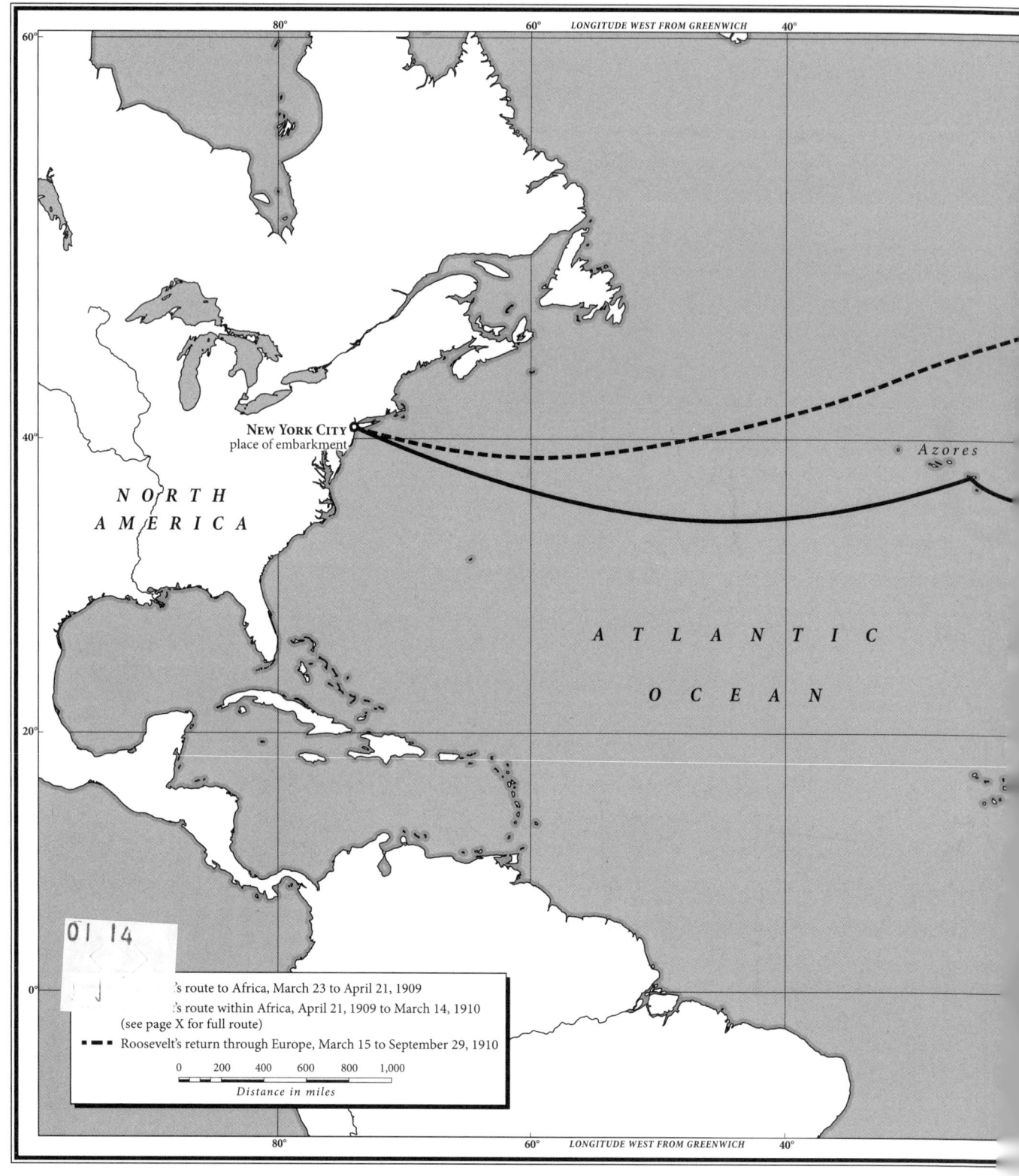

80°   60°   *LONGITUDE WEST FROM GREENWICH*   40°

60°

40°

NEW YORK CITY
place of embarkment

N O R T H

A M E R I C A

A T L A N T I C

O C E A N

Azores

20°

0°

's route to Africa, March 23 to April 21, 1909

's route within Africa, April 21, 1909 to March 14, 1910
(see page X for full route)

Roosevelt's return through Europe, March 15 to September 29, 1910

0   200   400   600   800   1,000

Distance in miles

80°   60°   *LONGITUDE WEST FROM GREENWICH*   40°